SLAIN
ABROAD

THE TRAGIC STORIES OF IRISH WHO
MET VIOLENT DEATHS FAR FROM HOME

MICHAEL O'TOOLE (40) has been Crime Correspondent for the *Irish Daily Star* since March 2000. He specialises in reporting on gangland Ireland, terrorism and sex offenders.

He has previously written books on the mystery of missing English girl Madeleine McCann, the life and death of gangster Eamon "The Don" Dunne and Irish domestic killings. He also co-wrote the best-selling book Black Operations: The Secret War Against The Real IRA.

He is married with three young children.

A journalist for nine years, **FIONA HYNES** (30) graduated from Dublin Institute of Technology with a BA in Journalism in 2002.

She was appointed News Editor with the *Irish Daily Star Sunday* in 2006, before returning to the *Irish Daily Star* as a news reporter in 2011.

SLAIN
ABROAD

THE TRAGIC STORIES OF IRISH WHO
MET VIOLENT DEATHS FAR FROM HOME

By Michael O'Toole and Fiona Hynes

ACKNOWLEDGEMENTS

Michael O'Toole wishes to thank all the people whose interviews, on and off the record, provided a basis for this book. Many people cannot be named, as they spoke in confidence, but their help is much appreciated.

I also wish to thank Amy Fitzpatrick's parents, Audrey and Christopher, Celine Conroy's parents Davey and Sandra, and all of Kelly Ann Corcoran's family, including her sister Caroline and brother-in-law Peter Moran.

Thanks also go to Jim Walpole, Gary Ashe and Mick O'Neill, three *Star* photographers who worked on these cases with me.

Fiona Hynes would like to thank the many people who gave up their time to make this book possible.

Particular thanks go to Lynsey O'Brien's mother, Sandra, Ruth McCourt's brothers, Ronnie and Mark Clifford, and Martin Coughlan's widow Catherine and daughter Denise.

Last but not least we wish to thank *The Star's* Chief Reporter Patrick O'Connell for his assistance and expertise in documenting the harrowing case of Michaela Harte.

Published in Ireland in 2011 by Paperweight Publications
Level 5, Building 4
Dundrum Town Centre
Sandyford Road
Dundrum, Dublin 16

ISBN   9780956913425

Paperweight

CONTENTS

FOREWORD

THE sudden death of a loved one is always a devastating experience. Whether the end is a tragic accident, or by the hand of another, the pain and anguish for those left behind is incalculable.

Somehow, though, when lives are lost beyond Irish shores, the sense of powerlessness and hopelessness is amplified all the more.

The cases contained in this book focus on some of Ireland's most notable deaths abroad.

Some victims were enjoying holidays of a lifetime when, in the blink of an eye, disaster struck.

Young mum Celine Conroy was brutally beaten to death by her partner in a Spanish holiday villa — while her children watched helplessly.

Teenager Lynsey O'Brien was on a Caribbean cruise with her family when, after a fateful night's drinking, she fell overboard off the coast of Mexico. Her body has never been recovered and her family have revealed how they still struggle to deal with her senseless passing.

Fellow Irish teenager Phoebe Prince met a different, but

equally tragic end, when she moved to America's east coast. The Co Clare schoolgirl was subjected to a horrific campaign of bullying at her new school that ultimately led her to end her own life.

Tragic Kelly Ann Corcoran met a horrific end at the hands of her husband Dermot McArdle, plummeting from the balcony of their hotel room.

And the murder of tragic newlywed Michaela McAreavey on her honeymoon in Mauritius shocked the entire nation.

Some deaths happen in such bizarre circumstances that the mystery threatens never to be solved.

Such a case is that of Tipperary man Michael Dwyer, who died in a hail of bullets in South America. Bolivian forces killed him after an alleged assassination attempt on the president was foiled — but his family insist their son could not have been involved in such activity.

The family of Trevor O'Keeffe had to wait long, painful years before the horrific story of his murder by French serial killer Pierre Chanal in 1987 finally came to light.

And then there are the mysteries that we still hope will have a happier conclusion — like that of Amy Fitzpatrick, the Irish teen who went missing in Spain in 2008. Her family has never given up hope that their girl will return to them.

Others stories featured in this book focus on Irish nationals who had ventured to foreign shores to carve out a life for themselves — only to be met by violent tragedy.

Aid worker Margaret Hassan devoted herself to helping the needy of Iraq. But not even an Irish passport could save her when militant gunmen took her hostage. They later beheaded her and broadcast the stomach-churning footage.

The 9/11 terrorist attacks sent ripples around the globe. Almost 3,000 people lost their lives — including six Irish people who had emigrated to the US to chase their dreams.

But not all emigrants were so innocent — gangland thugs Shane Coates and Stephen Sugg of the infamous Westies gang were gunned down while trying to build a drugs empire on Spain's Costa Del Crime.

These are their stories.

CELINE CONROY:
Hell at holiday villa

THERE was nothing they could do to save her.

As the crazed attacker brutally assaulted their defenceless mum, an eight-year-old boy and his five-year-old sister watched on, helpless.

They were only a matter of feet away as blow after blow rained down on her.

In the end, desperate, they resorted to begging.

Their pleas, however, fell on stonily deaf ears. The attacker kept kicking, punching and biting their mum Celine Conroy, even as she lay prone on the floor.

The attack was so vicious, so animalistic, that the life blood slowly drained out of her as he continued his vicious onslaught.

Twenty-six-year-old Celine didn't even have a chance to defend herself. It's likely the attacker knocked the Dublin mum-of-three out with the first punch, delivered to the side of her head as she stood at the stove of her holiday villa near Alicante on Spain's east coast.

That first blow was only the first of dozens — all within sight of two of Celine's three kids, Shane and Chloe.

Her third child Leah, who was just two at the time of the attack, was asleep in the main bedroom — blissfully unaware of what was happening to her mammy just a few feet away.

But for her other two kids, there was no escaping the events unfolding in front of their young and terrified eyes.

It's impossible to imagine the terror they must have felt as they watched the most important person in the world to them suffering so badly.

And to make their ordeal even more traumatic, the attacker was not some crazy burglar or serial killer.

It was the second most important person in the world: the man they called daddy.

Just two months earlier, Celine, partner Paul Hickey and the three kids left their flat in Sean Treacy House, a complex on north inner city Dublin's Buckingham Street, for a long holiday in San Fulgencio.

Hickey's father, convicted drug dealer Paul "Gash" Ainscough from Darndale in north Dublin, made a fortune from selling heroin in his native city in the 1980s.

Although he largely disappeared from the trade in the 1990s and first decade of this century, he had enough cash from his dealing days to buy the apartment in San Fulgencio — valued at around €300,000.

He let Hickey and Celine take the apartment, some 25 miles south west of Alicante for the summer of 2005.

Celine was a recovering drug addict, who had not taken heroin in several years.

Hickey, however, was still using all sorts of drugs — including heroin. He wanted to stay in Spain as it meant he could have easier access to the drugs he craved.

Celine, on the other hand, wanted desperately to go back to her native Dublin, especially as she needed to get a fresh batch of her prescription of heroin substitute methadone.

The tension between the pair led to frequent rows — which often ended in Hickey, a convicted criminal like his father, beating Celine.

But this time it was different. This time Hickey didn't stop. Not even the presence of his two eldest kids, and their pleas, had any effect on him.

"Stop it daddy, please stop it," they begged their father — and Celine's first and only love — as he beat her.

But Paul Hickey didn't even notice them through his drink and drugs induced rage.

Instead, he merely kept up the degrading assault until he could beat her no more.

Then, he made the children walk past their mum's body as he ordered them into the main bedroom, where little Leah was sleeping.

He then went and washed his hands, before joining the kids in the bedroom.

He was so high on a cocktail of drugs and alcohol that he was asleep on the bed within a few minutes.

It's unclear how long the two eldest kids stayed awake, but they eventually drifted off to sleep.

The full horror of what happened that night only came to light at around 12 noon the next day.

A few days earlier, Hickey's aunt Nora Armitage and her son Aaron had joined him and Celine at the villa, on Calle Helsinki in the resort of San Fulgencio, around 25 miles south west of Alicante.

Ms Armitage was living with Aaron and her husband Glynn on the Isle of Man, but was close to Paul Hickey's family.

On the Wednesday two days before the attack, an already aggressive Hickey was becoming increasingly unstable.

He drove Aaron to a nearby town where he was due to pick up medication for a minor ailment. As Aaron went into the doctor's surgery, Hickey suddenly drove off — leaving the teenager alone in a strange country, with no money and no phone to ring his mother.

On the Friday, hours before he turned on Celine, he became even more unpredictable. Celine told him she did not want to accompany him on a night out to a local karaoke bar with Nora and Aaron.

He threatened her and forced her to dress up for a night out and parade up and down outside the house. Then, callously, he told her he had changed his mind and she could get changed.

Nora Armitage and Aaron left the house at around 8pm. They walked into the local town and returned at roughly 11pm.

By this stage, unknown to them, Hickey had already meted out the brutal assault and the villa was in complete darkness.

Aaron and Nora knocked and banged on the door — but there was no reply. They were forced to sleep on the terrace of the villa, using cushions from sun loungers as pillows.

The next morning, the pair went next door to an English couple who had a spare key. Just after midday, Nora unlocked the front door.

What she saw will stay with her until the end of her days. Celine was lying in the centre of the living room. She was clearly dead and the towel Hickey had draped on her was still in place.

Deeply traumatised, Nora had a sickening thought: what if the kids were dead as well? Frantically, she ran to the master bedroom. There, she saw Hickey flat out cold on the bed, the two older kids beside him and Leah in her cot.

It was early in the evening of Saturday, August 27, 2005, and life would never be the same again for anyone who was in that villa.

Within seconds of making the grim discovery, Nora alerted the English neighbours, who made an emergency call to the Spanish Guardia Civil.

Officers arrived at the scene within minutes. By the

time they arrived Hickey was awake. He was shouting and rampaging around the house again.

The police held back for reinforcements for almost an hour until the neighbours explained there were children inside. Two officers immediately went in and rescued the kids.

Dealing with Hickey, however, was another matter. He was frantically thrashing around and was simply unmanageable.

Eventually, up to a dozen burly Guardia Civil officers had to come together to face him down. They only managed it with the help of a doctor, who injected him with a sedative.

While he was being carted off to the local Guardia Civil station, frantic phone calls were being made back to Ireland — to Celine's and Hickey's families.

Celine's mother Sandra Conroy, only recently diagnosed with cancer, was one of the first to hear the heartbreaking news. Within hours, Celine's father Davey Conroy and other family members were on a flight to Alicante from Dublin.

In an ironic twist, Hickey's father, drug dealer Gash Ainscough, was on the same flight with members of his family.

The following day, Mr Conroy had a task that no parent should ever have: Spanish cops asked him to identify Celine's battered body. With Celine's uncle David Fitzsimons, he went to the morgue for the gruesome task.

But Hickey had left his beloved daughter in such a horrible state that at first he didn't recognise her.

"We lifted the sheet and said 'That's not her'," Mr Fitzsimons recalled. "We asked and they brought us back and showed us the name tag — Conroy.

"Then we saw the ring that [Celine's cousin] Maria gave her, that she always wore. Davey grabbed hold of me and held on so hard I thought I had a cracked rib.

"The man was inconsolable. He didn't recognise her, neither of us did. Celine had blonde hair, but when we saw her it was grey and covered in blood. We asked about it and they said that was because of the shock of what he did to her."

Hickey was quickly taken from the Guardia Civil station to a psychiatric hospital, where he was held for several days before being brought to court in Orihuela, close to Alicante. He wore shorts, a sports singlet and runners as he was led handcuffed into the court after being driven there face-down in the back of a police car.

Under the Spanish system, suspects are not charged immediately, even if, like Hickey, there is a massive amount of hard evidence against him. Instead, they are told they are being placed under formal investigation by a magistrate. A judge can either release them on bail or order their detention.

In Hickey's case, the judge ordered that he be locked up until he was ready to stand trial, at which stage he would be formally charged. He was taken to the notorious Fontcalent Prison, close to Alicante, where he would await his trial date.

While the short court hearing was taking place, Mr Conroy was organising the return to Ireland of Celine's three kids.

But they would be going home without their beloved mum. Because the investigation into Celine's murder was so complex, Spanish officials refused to release her body.

Eventually, after much lobbying by her family, Celine's remains were finally allowed home to Ireland — more than two months after her death.

For Sandra, it was a bittersweet moment. She was still reeling from the murder, but was relieved to be getting Celine back home relatively quickly. The family had initially been told Spanish cops wanted to keep her body for up to a year.

However, they finally relented and allowed her to be flown back home in the second week of October. Ms Conroy told *The Star* at the time: "It's a great relief that Celine is finally coming home. We'll be up at the airport at 11.30am to see her coming back.

"We were worried that she would have to stay in Spain for up to a year. But last week the Spanish said she could come home. They were waiting on forensic reports and they got them, but I also think that they allowed Celine home because they know I'm so sick."

Ms Conroy's brother Thomas was on the flight that brought Celine home. "We didn't want her to come home alone,"

Sandra said.

With her body home at last, her family could finally say goodbye to her. Celine's funeral took place on October 19 — almost eight weeks after her murder. Hundreds of people packed into Our Lady of Lourdes Church in north Dublin's Sean McDermott Street for the heartbreaking ceremony.

Shane and Chloe, whose last sight of their mother was of her being beaten and kicked to death, placed a handmade card on her coffin, just in front of the altar.

"We miss you mammy," Chloe wrote, "I hope heaven is a nice place and you are having a good time. We love you, xx."

Leah sat playing on the floor beside the altar during the service – oblivious to what was happening around her.

As the immaculately dressed Chloe and Shane carried gifts to the altar before the offertory, it was simply too moving a sight for many of the congregation who broke down in tears.

Sandra clutched a pink rose to her chest as she led the mourners. Celine's aunt Patricia, who lives in England, told the church her niece lived for her babies.

"All Celine wanted was her children," Patricia said. "She loved her children and she loved Paul since she was 14. He told me he would look after her. Now she is in heaven."

Celine's coffin was taken from the church to the Celine Dion song Immortality. She was later buried in the same grave at Glasnevin cemetery as her grandparents Patty and Tommy Fitzsimons. Celine's uncle Darren, who died when he was just 17, is also buried in the same grave. "She regarded him as a brother," Ms Conroy said.

The long wait to have Celine home and given a Christian burial had finally come to an end. But the Conroy family would have to wait more than three years to see something else they were desperately yearning for.

That's how long it would be before Paul Hickey was finally brought to justice for what he did.

Early on the morning of November 12, 2008, Sandra, her husband Davey and other members of the Conroy family walked together into a drab, grey office building in the town of Elche, 13 miles from Alicante.

As they waited to go through the airport-style security scanner, they knew that the day they had longed for was finally here. In a few minutes, they would come face to face with Hickey for the first time since the murder.

He had been in prison for the previous three years — but now his trial for the murder of Celine could begin.

Spanish prosecutors have the right, even before a trial starts, to demand a fitting penalty for when the accused is convicted. In Hickey's case, the prosecution team did not hold back.

It claimed that Hickey assaulted Celine at 9pm, but she was still alive when he finished his assault — and did not in fact die until 4am the following day.

They claimed rather than getting her help when he realised she was in mortal danger, he simply walked out of the living room and left her to die.

And they argued Hickey continued beating her after he knew he had used enough violence to kill her, stating: "Most of the blows delivered by Hickey were unnecessary to attain his goal of killing Celine Conroy.

"But he continued to beat her forcefully and deliberately to increase her suffering," the prosecution document alleged.

A coroner's document prepared for the trial showed, for the first time, the true and shocking extent of the injuries that Celine suffered at the hands of Hickey.

Almost every part of her upper body was injured in the brutal attack – and she had 35 different injuries. They were: a 2cm cut on her right upper eyelid; a 2.5cm graze on her right cheek; a 4cm graze, also on her right cheek; a haematoma on each of her eye sockets; a bruise on her right forehead; bruising and swelling on the bridge of the nose; a 1.5cm bruise under her chin; bruising of the nose; a 1cm cut to the nose; another 1.5cm cut to the nose; a 1.5cm cut to the left upper eyelid; a massive bruise to the left half of her face; a cut to the left corner of her mouth; a cut to the lower left lip; bruising to both ears; bleeding from both ears; a lesion 4.5cm by 0.5cm on the right upper chest; a bruise to the upper right chest, measuring 3.5cm by 2cm; another bruise in the same area, again measuring 3.5cm by 2cm; a bruise between her breasts measuring 5cm by 3cm; a 2cm bruise to the left side of her throat; a swelling to her left collar bone; four irregular bruises down the right side of her torso; another bruise, this time 3cm long and in the shape of a half moon on her right side; bruising to the right abdomen; a bruise 3cm by 4cm to the pubic area; a 2cm gash to the left abdomen; bruising to the left buttock; an 0.5cm graze to her left ankle; a 3cm by 2cm bruise to her left forearm; a 4cm by 2cm bruise to her upper left arm; an 8cm by 2cm bruise on her right forearm; a 5cm by 4cm bruise on her right elbow; and all but two of her teeth had been beaten or kicked out of her upper jaw.

It's no wonder that, as she prepared for the trial to start and aware of the contents of the sickening coroner's report, Sandra thought 20 years for Hickey was simply not enough.

"I want him locked up for life and I want them to throw away the key. It should be life for a life," Ms Conroy told *The Star* before the case began. "He is nothing more than an animal, that's all he is. And I want him to serve his time as hard as possible," she said.

Hickey would soon show, however, that the term animal was probably too kind to describe him.

He was brought into the court building in a Guardia Civil van, which brought him to a side entrance and kept him away from Celine's family. He was kept in a side room for around three hours as fevered speculation gripped the 40 or so people present that he was going to change his plea.

Hickey had initially indicated that he was going to plead not guilty and blame the killing on a cocktail of drugs. But blood tests taken from him on the day after the murder clearly showed that there were no illegal narcotics in his system.

That significantly weakened his defence and, around 20 minutes before the trial was due to start, it became clear that he wanted to do a deal.

If he kept up the pretence that he was innocent, he would still be convicted and caged for 20 years. But at the last moment, he offered to plead guilty to the lesser charge of manslaughter — in return for a smaller sentence.

He would have to stand in court and admit his guilt, but would not be facing a 20 year jail term. Instead, he would be handed down a 15-year term. But that would be backdated to when he went into custody in August 2005 — and, with standard remission, Hickey would be free by 2015.

He grabbed the opportunity with both hands.

Just after 3pm, Hickey was brought into the underground courtroom where he was formally asked if he acknowledged that he had killed Celine. "I killed her but I did not mean to cause her any extra harm," he told the court.

 State prosecutor Pablo Romero told the court it accepted the plea bargain. "The accused admits causing her death, but denies the intention to extend her suffering. This was a killing, it was not a murder," he said.

Mr Romero then turned to Hickey and asked him: "Do you confess to causing her death?"

Hickey replied with just one word: "Yes."

He was then asked: "Do you confess to punching her until she fell to the ground?"

Again, he simply replied: "Yes."

The lawyer then asked: "Was it without premeditation?"

He once more replied " Yes."

But when he was asked: "Did you inflict more pain than was necessary to cause her death?," Hickey replied: "No."

But then Hickey did something that horrified and shocked everyone who was present that day.

Just minutes after admitting his guilt, he was brought out of the courtroom to be taken away to prison to begin his 15 year sentence. He had to walk past members of Celine's extended family — and started roaring abuse at them.

Hickey gave them the finger and told one of them "Shut your mouth..."

The sneering killer could clearly be seen laughing and smiling as he was led past up to 20 members of Celine's family, who launched their own tirade of abuse against him.

While Hickey was being led away to start his sentence in the notorious Villena Prison, Sandra and Davey Conroy were trying to come to terms with what had just happened.

They had waited more than three years for the trial, but in the end their daughter's life and death only took up a few hours of the Spanish judicial system.

Standing outside the court building, a clearly upset Sandra still had one unanswered question. She told reporters she just wanted to know what was behind the attack.

"Why did you do it Paul? Why?" she said. "I know we'll never get an answer, he's not man enough to give us an answer. I would love to ask him why he did it.

"Why did he do that to Celine, what did she do to deserve that? The kids said she did nothing. She was sick and he took her out of her sick bed. He kicked her like an animal and bit her like an animal. A horse would not have done to her what he did to her."

Sandra said the family's priority was now to look after Celine's three kids Shane (then 12), Chloe (9) and Leah (5). And she paid an emotional tribute to her daughter.

"She was just an ordinary girl who loved her children, loved him — he was her only boyfriend ever, her first love, her only love and that's the way he treated her," Sandra said. "She lived for her children, she lived for her one holiday every year.

"She was my shadow, she's gone now and I'll never be able to get her back. You may all forget about her, but I never will, I never can. We will never be the same without her."

Two days later, Hickey gave Sandra her answer.

The Star managed to get into Villena Prison and interviewed Hickey for almost an hour. It was the first time he had ever spoken publicly about the events of that night in August 2005.

He revealed how Shane and Chloe begged him to stop — but he ignored them. "All I can remember is the kids shouting, 'Stop it Daddy, please stop it'," he admitted.

But Hickey insisted he had no idea why he attacked her in the first place. He said: "I loved Celine and I still do. I can think of only two other times where we had a physical fight — we really loved each other."

Hickey insisted he had gone days without sleeping before the killing — and on the day itself had taken cocaine, cannabis, tranquillizers and alcohol, although court documents said there was only a mild sedative.

"I had not been sleeping for days and I could hear voices in my head," Hickey said. "Everywhere I went I could see people looking at me. Everyone was.

"On the night it happened, I felt terrible and went to a cafe nearby where I got a big glass of Hennessy (brandy). That must have had something to do with it.

"I went back up to the house and Celine was there.

He said: "I didn't mean to kill her — it was an accident. My mind just went blank after I hit her the first time. I just lost it.

"I'll never be able to explain why I did it because there was no reason for it. I can remember hitting her a punch, the both of us ending up on the floor and the kids screaming at me to stop. But Celine never said a word — I must have knocked her out with the first punch."

Even though Hickey subjected Celine to a brutal death, he still claimed she was the love of his life. "I'm really, truly sorry for what I did," he said. "I still love her and always will.

"I want everyone to know that I am really, really sorry for killing her — I can't believe I did it myself. My lawyer told me I used repeated blows against her and I have to accept it. I saw the photographs of what I did to her — I couldn't even recognise her. Her face was all purple. It was terrible."

He then spoke of the moment he turned on her. He recalled: "I went back up to the house and Celine was there.

"I started cooking and then asked her if she would do it for me. She said something like, 'Yeah, I will now'. There was no aggression or anything from her.

"But I just looked at her and said, 'What did you say?' and went up to her. I punched her once on the face and she went down.

"There was no reason for what I did. She didn't do anything to provoke me. My mind has gone blank after that, but I have been told I beat her for around 10 minutes.

"I can't remember anymore. All I can remember is the kids shouting, 'Stop it Daddy, please stop it'.

"I then told the kids to go into the bedroom and went and washed my hands. Then I went to sleep and the next thing I remember is a Guardia Civil fella waking me up."

Hickey said he was desperate to apologise to his kids for taking their mother away. "I want them to know that I am really, really sorry for killing her," he said.

"I didn't mean it. It was an accident. I loved her and I still do. I also want Celine's parents to know that I am apologising to them as well.

"I saw after I was in court that Sandra went on TV and asked my why I did it. But I don't have any reason for it — I just must have lost the head."

The visit ended after about 40 minutes when the guards turned off the phone into which he was speaking. But before he left, Hickey said: "I know what I did and I know I have to face up what I did forever."

While he was in the mood to apologise, he also said sorry to Celine's parents for his antics at the court. The image of him giving the finger and pouring abuse on Celine's family is one that will haunt anyone who witnessed it.

"I shouldn't have done that. I was playing up for the cameras a bit," Hickey conceded.

But although he was magnanimous in his apology, he could not help turning the conversation around to himself and his plight in Villena Prison. It is regarded as one of the most dangerous penitentiaries in Spain and sees more inmates being attacked inside than in any other jail in the country.

A report for the Spanish Justice Ministry also found that the jail, which was only opened in 2002, has had a massive number of staff being attacked or threatened by inmates.

The prison, around 40 miles from the spot where Hickey beat Celine Conroy to death, has more than 1,150 inmates and is one of the biggest in the country. In 2007 alone, there were 64 different attacks on inmates in the prison, home to rapists, murderers, paedophiles and gangsters.

The other prison in the Alicante area, called Fontcalent, only had five attacks on inmates in the same period. There were also 54 incidents of staff being attacked or threatened in the jail — which makes Villena the third most dangerous jail in the country for employees.

A spokesman for the Prison Officers union in Spain said violence inside Villena was now so bad that most staff regard fights and attacks as part of their normal work. The union also said inmates regularly make homemade weapons, including knives and pieces of metal. Villena also has an above average of suicides and attempted suicides amongst prisoners.

And it was clear when *The Star* spoke to Hickey in one of the visiting cubicles that he genuinely feared for his life.

"I see men having sex with each other all the time in the showers — it's terrible in here," he said. "One day my cell mate tried to rape me and I had to call the guards for help.

"Another time, a Spanish fella asked me for a fight. I said no and he came at with a knife. I managed to grab it, and he got my arm – but then he started stabbing me in the body. He stabbed me five times altogether.

"The Russians and Romanians asked me if I wanted them to sort the fella out, but I just said to leave it. This place is a hole. They'd kill you or rape you here no problems."

But his sentence will not last forever. With remission and the fact that he has been in custody since 2005, Hickey will be a free man in 2015.

And although he admitted responsibility for the callous killing, his family still love and cherish him. His mother Bridie speaks to him regularly on the phone and his father, convicted drug dealer Paul "Gash" Ainscough, is standing by him.

In fact, Ainscough is trying to mount a campaign to win his son's freedom — and is blaming the killing on the drugs he was taking.

"It wasn't Paul's fault, it was the drugs he was given," Ainscough said. "Paul is not a murderer. My son should not be in jail and Celine should not be dead. She should be with Paul and with her children."

Ainscough says he now has evidence that the drugs were to blame — not his killer son.

And Ainscough also says he has now kick-started a prosecution against the person he believes gave Hickey the drugs. "I will be mounting a prosecution," he said.

Ainscough claims his son should have been allowed to use the defence of automatism in his trial. This defence says that people cannot be held responsible for their actions if they had no control over what they did — including from the effects of taking substances.

But the chances of Hickey winning any appeal, or of Ainscough prosecuting the man he says gave his son the drugs, are tiny. The grim reality is that there is only one person to blame for Celine Conroy's brutal, horrific and violent death.

That is the person who kicked and punched her to death in front of two of her horrified kids.

That person is the thug who made the children walk past her lifeless body as she lay on the floor.

That person is the man who went and had a shower after killing her and then fell asleep in bed – oblivious or uncaring that Celine was dead just a few yards away.

That person is the man who laughed and sneered at Celine's family when he was facing justice for the killing.

That person is the person who, finally, said sorry what he had done — after putting her family through hell for more than three years.

That person is Paul Hickey.

MARGARET HASSAN:
The angel of Baghdad

IT WAS an agonising image — Irish aid worker Margaret Hassan crying and pleading for her life. Distressed and exhausted looking, Mrs Hassan stared into the camera, pleading for rescue, begging for help, saying this could be her final hour. Rescue, however, would never arrive.

This was how the world came to know of the brave Irish aid worker who was abducted in Iraq as she made her way to work. The angel of Baghdad, as Margaret had been affectionately called, had been living in the country for more than 30 years and was married to an Iraqi.

As director of Care International's charity in the country, she was a respected figure who had been accepted by the Iraqis as one of their own.

But when she was hauled out of her car by a gang of masked gunmen on the morning of October 19, 2004, and taken captive, not Margaret's charity work, nor her relationship with the Iraqi people, nor even her Irish passport, would be enough to save her life.

The Iraq of 2004 was a land gripped by strife. Following the successful invasion by British and US forces in 2003 and the toppling of dictator Saddam Hussein, the country was plunged into unrest with a multitude of insurgent groups taking up arms. Kidnapping and hostage taking became rife as groups vied for maximum publicity for their agenda, and funded their campaigns of terror from ransom payoffs.

Margaret's abduction was a watershed. She was the first female captive to be murdered by her kidnappers and the massive outpouring of anger and demands for her immediate release after her abduction demonstrated that this was no ordinary captive.

Far from being a stranger in a strange land, the Dublin native had called the Gulf state home for more than 30 years.

Born in Dalkey, Dublin, to parents Peter and Mary Fitzsimons, Margaret and her family moved to London soon after the end of World War Two and this was where her three sisters, Deirdre, Geraldine and Kathryn and her brother Michael were born. Embracing her role as big sister, Margaret was extremely close to all four of her siblings.

According to her family, Margaret's love of the Arab people started in the mid 1960s when she worked in Palestinian refugee camps in Lebanon. The experience of working with people suffering appalling living conditions, following a series of devastating wars with Israel, deeply moved Margaret, then a young woman in her 20s.

Her sister Geraldine Fitzsimons Riney, who lives in Kenmare, Co Kerry, explained: "Margaret had only goodwill towards everyone. She had no prejudice against any creed. She dedicated her whole life to working for the poor and vulnerable, helping those who had no-one else."

At the age of 27, Margaret married Tasheen Ali Hassan, a 29-year-old Iraqi man studying engineering in Britain and in 1972 the newlyweds moved to Iraq and settled in the capital Baghdad.

Margaret soon found work teaching English with the British Council in Iraq, a position that made her well-known among educated Iraqis. Tasheen, meanwhile, worked as an economist. During the 1980s Margaret became the assistant director of studies at the British Council, one of the world's largest English teaching organisations, and later in that decade was appointed director.

When war came in the form of the first Gulf War in 1991, sparked when Iraq invaded oil rich Kuwait, Margaret remained in the country with her husband.

However, the British Council suspended its operations and by the end of the conflict she was left without a job.

But in late 1991 Margaret was to find her real calling when she took up a job with the humanitarian relief charity, Care International, who had just established themselves in the country with the initial aim of helping Kurdish refugees.

Following the first Gulf War, Iraq was hit by draconian economic sanctions enforced by the United Nations. Sanitation, health, and nutrition became major concerns.

Margaret instantly took up opposition against these sanctions, and became a vocal critic.

The war and UN sanctions had left Iraqis without one of the most basic necessities of human life — water.

Water and sewage plants were in disrepair and the fractured water system led to very high levels of water intoxication and diseases. Under Margaret's direction, Care, founded in the US in 1945, began to focus its attention on restructuring and maintaining water systems in central and southern Iraq, while also helping to feed children in hospitals.

Margaret devoted her life to helping the situation of ordinary Iraqis directing projects involving water, sanitation and health care, and helped an estimated 17 million people during her time in the country. But she did so without the need or desire for public affirmation. Colleagues said she never liked people to know and talk about a good deed she had done.

Esteemed Iraqi writer, Abdul Qadir Ahmed, who was a friend of Margaret, said about her: "The most interesting thing about her was when she helped a certain place or when she reconstructed a certain hospital; unlike other organisations, she would refuse to mark the emblem of her organisation or to have it publicised.

"I have never seen anyone so truthful to their pledges and promises as Margaret was. I have not seen anyone who wished well for Iraq as much as Margaret did. I have not seen anybody who liked to help the disabled and the helpless as much as she did, and who loved their job equally as much."

Another friend, film-maker Felicity Arbuthnot, documented some of Margaret's work, and described her as an "extraordinary person". She said she once travelled with Margaret to a water sanitation plant in a poor area of Iraq and witnessed her effect on the local people she was helping.

"A crowd gathered and tiny children rushed up and threw their arms round her knees, saying, 'Madam Margaret, Madam Margaret,' and everywhere she went, people just beamed. She was so loved and everybody was so open with her."

While Margaret continued with her good work, storm clouds were once more gathering over Iraq and in 2002 talk had begun about a new war between the US and Iraq.

As opposed as ever to conflict, Margaret travelled to Britain to speak out about the war and meet with members of the British Parliament to advise them against joining the invasion. There she warned British politicians that Iraq could face a humanitarian catastrophe in the event of a conflict. She said UN sanctions had left the Iraqi people in a worse situation than they had been at the end of the first Gulf War in 1991.

"The Iraqi people are already living through a terrible emergency," she told a House of Commons briefing. "They do not have the resources to withstand an additional crisis brought about by military action."

In the lead up to the conflict, Margaret, who was at this stage director of Care International, was preparing to help install new water infrastructure in needy southern Iraq, where conditions had reached crisis levels.

She explained at the time: "In Hamza and Mahaweel the hospitals were in terrible state of repairs — parts were actually crumbling. Consultant doctors were working three in a room in the least-damaged parts of the buildings, trying to deal with patients. The water supply was inadequate and the hospitals had no sewage disposal. Raw sewage was flowing back into the river. The primary health centre was collapsing. We finally pulled it down."

But just as her charity got ready to begin work, Margaret was forced to delay the roll out of the new infrastructure, explaining that she wanted to delay installation "in anticipation of further developments in the region". Once more war was on her doorstep, and tragically Margaret would never get to oversee work on what was to be her final project.

Along with her husband, Tahseen, she chose to stay in Iraq during the 2003 war, and told a British newspaper on the eve of the conflict that she was "sad" Britain was taking part.

She added that she did not fear being targeted in revenge attacks by Iraqis. But this proved to be a fatally wrong assertion on Margaret's behalf because despite her great humanitarian record and years of selfless toil on behalf of ordinary Iraqis she did become a target.

Along with her Iraqi and Irish nationality, Margaret Hassan also had British citizenship and for the insurgents of Iraq, this made her a prominent and in their eyes, legitimate target. Margaret Hassan was about to pay the ultimate price.

The morning of October 19, 2004, started much like any other busy weekday for Margaret Hassan.

The country she loved and called home might have been gripped by conflict, but this did not stop her from working. She arranged for her driver to pick her up that morning and drive her across Baghdad to her office in the west of the city.

Her to-do list was growing ever higher as Iraqis suffered from the effects of yet more conflict and a slow response by the US to re-install electricity and water after the initial conflict with Saddam Hussein's forces ended.

As she prepared herself for a busy day, Margaret may not have even noticed the gunmen dressed as policemen as they had blocked the route of her car.

Just after 7.30am she was dragged from her vehicle,

blindfolded and thrown into the back of a waiting car, but it didn't take long for the alarm to be raised.

Hours later, video footage of Margaret, wearing a white blouse and with her hands bound behind her back, was shown on Arab TV station Al-Jazeera. She was in a whitewashed room and appeared distressed. The TV station reported that an unnamed "armed Iraqi group" had kidnapped her.

The very next day, her terrified husband, Tahseen, made an emotional appeal to the kidnappers to free her.

He told Al-Arabiya satellite television: "I would like to tell the kidnappers that we are in the holy month of Ramadan and my wife has been helping Iraq for 30 years and loved this country. In the name of humanity, Islam and brotherhood, I appeal to the kidnappers to free her because she has nothing to do with politics."

By this stage no ransom request had been delivered to authorities, which was unusual in itself as Margaret was one of the most high-profile victims to go missing in a spate of kidnappings that had rocked the city.

Scores of foreigners —from aid workers and engineers to fuel tank drivers had been abducted — with 35 known to have been killed. But her family and loved ones may have taken some comfort in the knowledge that insurgents had yet to kill any female captives.

Two Italian aid workers had been kidnapped weeks before, and had subsequently been released unharmed.

There were a string of reports afterwards that the Italian government, who had troops in the country, had paid about €1m to secure their release. But Britain, like the United States, were much firmer in their refusal to deal with hostage takers and no doubt lurking in the back of Margaret's relatives mind was the haunting image of Liverpool native, Kenneth Bigley.

Kenneth (62) was an engineer and had been contract working in Iraq in the aftermath of the US led invasion. He had been working for Gulf Supplies and Commercial Services, a Kuwaiti company working on reconstruction projects in Iraq.

On September 16, 2004, he was kidnapped along with

two colleagues, Americans Jack Hensley and Eugene Armstrong by the Tawhid and Jihad group led by the notorious Jordanian militant, Abu Musab al-Zarqawi.

Unlike Margaret, Mr Bigley and his companions had known their house was being watched and understood that they were in grave danger after their Iraqi house guard quit after revealing he had been threatened by militias.

Two days after they were seized, a video emerged from his kidnappers threatening to kill all three hostages in 48 hours if their demands to release female Iraqi prisoners were not agreed to. When the terrorists demands were not met, the first of the American prisoners, Eugene Armstrong, was beheaded. Some 24 hours later, Jack Hensley was murdered.

A few days later, Kenneth Bigley appeared on television again begging the then British Prime Minister Tony Blair to help him. Dressed in an orange jumpsuit and crouched down in a small chicken cage, he told the camera: "I need you to help me now, Mr Blair, because you are the only person on God's earth who can help me."

His 86-year-old mother, Lil, also went on TV pleading for her son to be released and collapsed moments afterwards and had to be treated in hospital. During this period, Mr Bigley was granted an Irish passport in absentia based on the fact that his mother had been born in Dublin. It was hoped that by stressing his Irish connection, his life might be saved.

By the end of September 2004, then Taoiseach Bertie Ahern, Sinn Fein president Gerry Adams, and Labour's then spokesperson on Foreign Affairs, Michael D Higgins, had all appeared on Arab television station, Al-Jazeera, calling for Mr Bigley's release. Even Libyan leader Muammar Gaddafi got in on the act, appealing for Mr Bigley's kidnappers to let him go.

Amazingly, during the last few days of his near three-week captivity, Mr Bigley, managed to flee from his captors.

With the help of one of his kidnappers and some involvement from British spy agency, MI6, he managed to escape for more than half and hour. However, he was recaptured near the town of Latifiya, south-west Baghdad, having never made it close enough to the main street to call for help.

His fate was now sealed, and on October 8 news reports surfaced on Arab television that he was dead.

A video released by the kidnappers showed six hooded men standing behind Mr Bigley, who was on his knees. One of the six spoke in Arabic for a minute. He said the group would carry out the "sentence of execution against this hostage because the British government did not meet our demand" which had been to release Iraqi women held by the US-led command in the country. The man then took a knife from his belt and cut off Mr Bigley's head as three other militants held him down.

The killer then held up the head for the camera. Mr Bigley's death was met with utter revulsion and widely condemned. His Thai-born wife of eight years, Sombat, who had also made several appeals for his release, spoke of her devastation revealing that the engineer was captured just weeks before his official retirement when he had been due to join her in Thailand.

Some weeks after his death, US forces discovered the chicken wire in which Mr Bigley had been kept in a house in the Iraqi town of Fallujah. The US military stated that in 20 houses it found paraphernalia associated with hostage-taking and torture, including shackles, blood-stained walls, and a torture chamber. However, Mr Bigley's body has never been found — although it has been claimed that he is buried in a ditch close to the entrance to Fallujah.

With the images of Mr Bigley's horrific murder fresh in their minds, Margaret's loved ones began their own campaign to try and force her captors to release her. Time was very much of the essence.

Care International immediately announced a halt to its operations in Iraq following the abduction — pending Margaret's safe release.

Former Taoiseach Bertie Ahern told the Dail that everything was being done to fight for Margaret's release, saying it was a "terrible deed" to inflict on her family.

"All communication links are being used. It is very important that people know she is Irish. That may not have been known. We have to stand up for our own," he added.

Former Foreign Affairs Minister Dermot Ahern rang Tahseen Hassan to express the solidarity of the Irish people.

While all of this was going on, Irish embassy staff in the region were hard at work behind the scenes — stressing Margaret's Irish background and trying to help in finding a way to have her released.

On October 21, Tahseen made a second appeal to the kidnappers to free his wife. Later that day, colleagues of Margaret's said they were hopeful that she would be released and said an enormous amount of work was being done on the ground to try and secure her release. The fact that Margaret spoke fluent Arabic and could explain her work to her captors in their own language was also seen as a positive.

Privately, however, experts feared that the timing of Margaret's abduction did not bode well for her safety. Her kidnapping had coincided with an intensification of violence ahead of the US presidential elections which were due to take place the following month and the planned introduction of British troops to sensitive Sunni districts in south Baghdad.

Also, the manner in which she was abducted — forced from her car at gunpoint after it was intercepted en route to her workplace — spoke of a level of organisation not usually associated with criminal gangs involved in kidnapping and extortion. Rather, her abduction appeared to have been executed along the lines of a military operation involving elements of surveillance, reconnaissance and the type of mobile communications necessary to effect an apparently seamless carjacking in broad daylight in a heavily patrolled area.

The abduction also seemed to involve a calculated and carefully restrained use of force to "lift" the target physically unharmed.

The fact that Margaret's image, recorded on digital camera, appeared on Arabic news channels within hours of her kidnapping also pointed to the fact the those responsible fully understood the terror and propaganda effect of such images.

It soon became clear that the command and control elements of her abduction betrayed a sophistication normally associated with politically motivated resistance groups such as Abu Mus-ab al Zarqawi's Tawhid and Jihad organisations — the same group responsible for Kenneth Bigley's murder a few weeks earlier.

On October 22 a new, harrowing video emerged of Margaret. In it she was weeping and begged Tony Blair to save her life by halting the deployment of 850 British troops from southern Iraq alongside US forces.

Margaret was seen begging to be spared the same fate as Kenneth Bigley. Breaking down in tears as she spoke, she said in a faltering voice: "Please help me, please help me. This might be my last hours. Please, the British people, ask Tony Blair to take the troops out of Baghdad and not to bring them to Baghdad. That's why people like Mr Bigley and myself are being caught and maybe we will die like Mr Bigley. Please, please, I beg you."

Her terrified husband Tasheen responded to the tape by saying that the then UK prime minister would have "blood on his hands" if his wife was murdered.

He said: "Margaret is now paying the price. Once they started talking in London about how they were going to rescue her, the kidnappers knew they could use her to apply pressure. I hold Tony Blair responsible for what is happening now. He used her kidnapping for propaganda. I have nothing now but the worst fears. I have been telling myself that they will not kill a woman, but I am no longer sure. I am so afraid and I am so sad. I feel very angry about Tony Blair. Margaret and I have tried to make sure even before the kidnapping that she was not considered British because there is so much hatred against America and Britain here because of the invasion."

The angel of Baghdad

A day later Tahseen made another appeal begging for his wife to be released saying, "It was very painful to see my wife crying," he said. As calls for Margaret's release continued to grow, Christian worshippers in Iraq prayed for her release and leading Muslim figures joined in the calls for her release, describing her kidnapping as something close to heresy.

Secretary general of Care International Denis Caillaux said of Margaret: "She is a naturalised Iraqi citizen and always holds the people of Iraq in her heart."

Some 200 people, many helped by Margaret, rallied at Care International's Baghdad office. They carried pictures of "Mama Margaret" and called for her captors to set her free.

Then something rather remarkable happened. The combined resistance groups of Fallujah, the destination for the majority of kidnapping victims in and around Baghdad, condemned Margaret's abduction and demanded her release.

Commanders of five separate guerrilla groups in Fallujah, which at that point was under rebel control, said they were not holding Margaret and had seen no evidence that Abu Musab al-Zarqawi's group were holding her either.

On October 27, a third video was released of a tired looking Margaret standing in a dimly lit room. In the video she urged Britain to withdraw its troops and free Iraqi women prisoners. Margaret also called on Care International to end their operations in Iraq. The charity responded by pulling out all of its staff — they have never returned. Unlike several other hostage videos, there were no banners or militants belonging to the still unnamed group appearing in the short footage.

As Margaret's family and husband became even more desperate a fourth shocking video emerged on November 2 in which her kidnappers threatened to turn her over to Abu Musab al-Zarqawi's group in 48 hours if their demands for troop withdrawals were not met immediately.

Arabic television station Al-Jazeera declined to broadcast the images of Margaret on humanitarian grounds. But it aired the second part showing a hooded man demanding that British troops be withdrawn from Iraq. Details about the content of the tape emerged in due course with the initial part of the video showing Margaret pleading for her life directly in front of the camera before fainting. A bucket of water was then believed to have been thrown over her head and she was filmed lying wet and helpless on the ground before getting up and crying.

It had now been more than two weeks since Margaret's abduction and hopes that she might be released unharmed were starting to fade. Realising their sister was in the gravest of danger, Margaret's brother and three sisters met with Bertie Ahern. Afterwards Mr Ahern, surrounded by Margaret's siblings, made a fresh appeal.

"Margaret is an Irish-born woman who has spent the last 30 years in Iraq. She has made her home there, marrying an Iraqi man even becoming a proud Iraqi citizen herself. During her time there, Margaret has devoted herself to the welfare and support of all the Iraqi people. Through her humanitarian work she has helped countless numbers of Iraqis," Mr Ahern said.

"She has worked tirelessly and selflessly on their behalf. Since Margaret was abducted some two weeks ago her husband and her family have endured enormous distress.

"I cannot imagine the trauma that Margaret herself has experienced. Margaret has no political associations. She represents no-one except the vulnerable and the poor.

"Your quarrel is not with Margaret. Nor is it with the Irish people who have been a firm friend of the Arab nation. So, I appeal to you, on behalf of the Irish people, on behalf of her Irish family, to release Margaret and allow her to return to her husband."

In response to the last video of Margaret, in which her captors threatened to turn her over to Abu Musab al-Zarqawi, al Qaeda in Iraq called for her release and promised to free her if she fell into their hands. In a message posted on the internet, the group which was now being led by al-Zarqawi, said it wanted the world to know that "if the kidnappers handed us this captive, we will release her immediately unless it is proven that she was conspiring against Muslims". The authenticity of the message could not be verified but it appeared on a website known for posting messages from Islamic militants.

Al-Jazeera said it received another tape of Margaret, which it refused to broadcast. In it she was coerced into claiming that she gave information to American officers at Baghdad Airport. A man's voice prompts her to keep to a text. "I admit that we worked with the occupation forces…" she says. Everyone connected to Margaret has denied that these claims were true, insisting she would never have spied on Iraqis.

After this, the trail went cold and for the next few days nothing more was heard from Margaret until November 11 when rumours began to circulate that evidence of a hostage murder had been discovered.

On November 14, the mutilated remains of a female woman were found in Fallujah, lying on the street under a blood-soaked cloth. US forces who discovered the remains said they were "80 per cent certain" that it was the body of a westerner and revealed the victim had blond hair unlike Margaret who had brown hair. At the time there was some speculation that it could be the body of Polish woman, Teresa Borcz Khalifa, who had also been taken hostage. But the Polish woman later turned up alive and well in her native country.

But any relief felt by Margaret's loved ones was short-lived as two days later her family said that they believed she was dead after being sent a video apparently showing her murder.

The video was sent to Al-Jazeera who decided it would never be broadcast. But details of aid worker Margaret's tragic last moments have since been revealed.

She stood in an empty room, blindfolded, awaiting her execution. Dressed in a white blouse, her head slightly bowed, a man approaches her from behind holding a pistol.

He points it at her head and places what appears to be an apple over the muzzle — to act, perhaps, like a primitive form of silencer. He then squeezes the trigger. There is a click, an apparent misfire, and the man retreats to the right of the screen and then reappears.

Margaret doesn't move although she must have heard the click. The man is wearing a grubby grey and black checked shirt and ill-fitting, baggy trousers and a scarf concealing his face. This time the gun fires and Margaret makes a tiny crying sound and falls backwards onto the ground landing on a plastic sheet. The camera lingers on her. It is over. Margaret Hassan, the angel of Baghdad is dead.

Afterwards Margaret's sisters and brother issued a statement, saying: "Our hearts are broken. We have kept hoping for as long as we could, but now we have to accept that Margaret has probably gone and at last her suffering has ended.

"Those who are guilty of this atrocious act, and those who support them, have no excuses. Nobody can justify this. Margaret was against sanctions and the war. To commit such a crime against anyone is unforgivable. But we cannot believe how anyone could do this to our kind, compassionate sister. The gap she leaves will never be filled."

Her heartbroken husband bravely read his statement to the cameras, begging for her remains to be returned to him.

"I have been told that there is a video of Margaret that appears to show her murder," he said. "The video may be genuine but I do not know. I beg those people who took Margaret to tell me what they have done with her. They can tell me. They can call the helpline. I need her. I need her back to rest in peace. Margaret lived with me in Iraq for 30 years. She dedicated her life to serving the Iraqi people. Please now. Please return her to me."

In the days after the release of the video, mourners gathered in Kenmare, Co Kerry, where Margaret's sister Geraldine and members of her extended family still live.

At the ecumenical service, parish priest Fr Tom Crean said her death had pierced "to the marrow of all our beings".

"Our hearts just cry out in pain with Margaret's family," he said, adding they would pray for the return of her body so people could "fully honour and celebrate her life".

Responding to the news of her death, Tony Blair said it was "abhorrent", while Bertie Ahern said her kidnappers "stand condemned by… the entire international community".

The following month a funeral Mass, which her grieving husband was too ill to attend, was held in London's Westminster Cathedral. As Margaret's body had still not been recovered, a picture of her was placed by the altar. A message from her family read during the service said: "She was brave, she was charitable, she was humble and hardworking. Yes, she was all of these things, but most of all she was our big sister."

Iraqi forces carried out a series of raids in south east Baghdad in May 2005 and arrested 11 people in relation to Margaret's killing. Police said they found ID, clothing and a handbag belonging to Margaret.

In the run up to the trial of three of the men held in connection with Margaret's death, her family revealed that they begged Britain's then foreign secretary Jack Straw to arrange for the men — who were arrested by US military — to be interviewed by British military police.

Margaret's sister, Deirdre Fitzsimons, said that the three men who were due to stand trial in Baghdad "know where my sister is buried".

"They were found with my sister's personal belongings, her handbag, her make-up, things that women carry around. These men know where my sister is buried and, all we have left, all we want to do now, is to bring her home."

But her pleas for British officials to interview the men were refused. "They have refused this request even though this is the only way that Margaret's remains will be found and we can bring her home to be buried with the dignity she deserves," she added.

Deirdre also revealed the family's belief that Margaret was killed because the UK government refused to speak to her hostage-takers. She revealed how kidnappers made four calls to her husband, Tahseen, asking to speak to the British embassy. Britain's Foreign Office confirmed he was called from her phone, but could not verify the caller's kidnapping claims.

"During the time of her captivity, four calls were made from the kidnappers to her husband Tahseen in Baghdad. These calls were made from Margaret's mobile phone," Deirdre said.

"The hostage-takers demanded to speak to a member of the British embassy, but Tahseen had been told by the British that they would not speak to the kidnappers. We believe the refusal by the British government to open a dialogue with the kidnappers cost our sister her life.

"The advice given to my brother-in-law was 'we'll emphasise her Iraqiness' — which was a ridiculous thing to do, after all, because they had kidnapped her in possession of her British passport. Margaret, who was vocally opposed to the war in Iraq, was sacrificed for the political ends of Tony Blair and George W Bush."

On June 5, 2006, an Iraqi man, Mustafa Mohammed Salman al-Jabouri was jailed for life in connection with Margaret's kidnapping. Two other men were acquitted. Al-Jabouri appealed and was given an 18-month sentence. In a statement, Margaret's family said the verdict left them "devastated and appalled. We feel Margaret has been betrayed".

Following further arrests, a second man, Ali Lutfi Jassar, was jailed for life in Baghdad in 2009 for his role in the kidnapping gang that murdered Margaret.

He was alleged to have contacted the British embassy in Baghdad demanding money in exchange for information revealing where Margaret's body was buried.

In communication with embassy officials, he mentioned an intimate detail about the aid worker that only her closest relatives and friends knew. He was seized by US special forces and Iraqi police investigating the extortion attempts.

Once again hopes were raised that Jassar, said to be a leading member in the kidnapping gang, would reveal details of her burial in exchange for a reduced sentence.

He avoided the death penalty and was sentenced to life in jail. Margaret's family welcomed the sentence but said they were bitterly disappointed that Jassar had not yet told them where Margaret was buried.

There was a further blow when a retrial was ordered after he claimed he was tortured into confessing and had in fact been out of the country at the time of her death.

Jassar, an English-speaking Sunni from Baghdad who called himself Abu Rasha, who had pleaded not guilty, said he had been beaten and given electric shocks during questioning.

"I have nothing to do with Hassan's abduction and I did not see or talk to her," he claimed.

Speaking at the time, Margaret's sister, Deirdre Manchanda, said: "We want Ali Lutfi Jassar to stay in prison because we are convinced he was definitely part of the kidnap gang because he knew too much to have got it from the internet or any other source.

"He has claimed many, many times in these transcripts to know where Margaret's remains are. We want to find our sister's remains because we want to bring her home to be buried and we want justice for her. It's not just justice for Margaret. It's justice for everybody. Apart from anything else, a terrorist murderer should not be on the streets of Baghdad."

Then, in August of last year, Jassar, the man who claimed to know where Margaret's remains were hidden escaped from Baghdad Central Prison, which is built on the site of the former Abu Ghraib, during prison riots in late 2009.

Iraqi deputy justice minister Busho Ibrahim confirmed the escape, saying: "People facilitated his escape. He is gone. He seized the opportunity of the riots in the prison in September 2009 and he escaped. He was the only one who escaped."

Despite attempts to track him down, his whereabouts remain a mystery and Margaret's family are left nursing the deepest of pains that their sister — who remained a practising Catholic her entire life — has not yet been given a dignified burial.

As for Margaret's husband, Tahseen, he remains in Baghdad, living out his retirement without the woman he chose to spend his life with. Still grief-stricken, he has been unable to watch the video of his wife's death. "I couldn't see the video that was released — not because she's my wife, but because I can't bear to see anyone assassinated," he said.

He remains deeply suspicious about who exactly was behind his wife's murder, saying in an interview in 2008: "I don't think insurgents did this. I don't think Iraqi people did this." But whether he ever gets to learn the truth about his beloved wife's murder remains to be seen.

TREVOR O'KEEFFE:
France's triangle of death

S HE was so close to justice she could almost touch it. As she sat in a small Parisian cafe, Eroline O'Keeffe knew that she was just minutes away from a conclusion to an epic battle she had fought for almost 18 years.

It was a battle in honour of her murdered son Trevor, who died at the hands of an infamous sexual sadist who terrorised much of northern France for almost a decade. And that made it one she simply could not, would not, lose.

It was a battle that saw the prime suspect for Trevor's gruesome murder — a highly experienced elite soldier and martial arts expert — implicated in at least seven other sex killings as well as up to 33 rapes of defenceless young men.

It was a battle that saw the suspect, who was at the heart of the French establishment, cheat justice by taking his own life just as he was about to stand trial for Trevor's murder.

And it was a battle that laid bare the French police's shambolic investigation into the suspect that — undoubtedly — cost several young men their lives.

And now that battle was almost over. All they had to do was wait 30 minutes.

On a cold winter's day on January 26, 2005, Eroline O'Keeffe and her sister Noeleen Slattery sat in the cafe across from the Palais De Justice, on the Boulevard Du Palais, right in the centre of Paris and a few hundred yards from the famous Louvre museum.

The Palais De Justice, or palace of Justice, was home to France's Superior Court — the equivalent of our High Court.

The palace itself is one of the most historic buildings in France. Justice has been handed down in Paris from this site for centuries, as far back as the 12th century. And from the 1500s to the French revolution in 1789, this was the home of the Paris parliament.

But it's unlikely the two Irish women had time to marvel at the architecture, such was their sense of expectation.

They had been told that Judge Jean-Claude Magendie of the Superior Court would deliver his verdict on a lawsuit taken by Ms O'Keeffe against the French state over its handling of the case against Pierre Chanal.

Ms O'Keeffe took the case because she was furious at negligence and delays in the investigation. She was horrified that French investigators had strong evidence in her son's case but failed to charge the suspect and then, incredibly, freed him on parole after he had been convicted of kidnapping and raping a Hungarian teenager.

Now all they had to do was wait until 2pm and they would hear the judge's verdict in Ms O'Keeffe's case. Just 30 minutes away.

But, while they were nervously sipping their coffees, the French state had yet another insult planned for them.

Judge Magendie strode into the imposing courtroom in the historic building and read out his judgement half an hour early.

The only people there to witness the judge's decision were three members of a French television crew, and a lawyer.

The courts had not even bothered to tell the relatives of the other men raped or murdered by Chanal that their compensation cases had been joined with Ms O'Keeffe's — so there was nobody directly involved in the litigation present to hear the outcome.

But if they had been there, they would have been delighted at the judge's words.

He didn't mince them. Judge Magendie accused the state of making serious and fundamental errors in its investigation into Chanal.

He said: "This series of errors significantly slowed down the investigation into several different disappearances [of young men]. It contributed to the continuing lack of identifying the circumstances of the kidnapping and murders of several victims."

"There were," he added, "numerous mistakes and instances of negligence. There was a denial of justice."

To make up for that lack of justice, Judge Magendie ordered that the French state pay Mrs O'Keeffe €25,000 in compensation, plus another €2,300 in legal bills.

He also ordered similar amounts be paid to the relatives of nine other men, murdered and buried by Chanal. In total, some 36 people received payouts, with more than €900,000 handed over by the French state.

It was a stunning victory for Ms O'Keeffe and the relatives of all the other victims of Chanal, a man now recognised as one of the most vicious and calculating serial killers France has ever seen.

The payments made front-page news in France and Ireland the next day — but for the families, the money was never an issue.

Much more important than cash, they wanted an acknowledgment by the French that they had been incompetent in their investigation — that young men were dead, their bodies never to be found, because of elementary mistakes.

"We have been awarded some money but nothing will ever bring Trevor back," Ms O'Keeffe said after the verdict. "But it is a victory of sorts because they have admitted that they were wrong. We knocked on doors again and again and demanded something be done.

"Eventually we forced them to bring the guilty man to trial. My only regret is they didn't stop his suicide. It was all about justice for Trevor. We have won a victory for him."

But it was a victory that came at a massive cost.

The French media called it the triangle of death.

Between January 1980 and April 1987 a small village in the north east of France became infamous as the site of the disappearance of seven young men.

Most of the men who vanished without trace were soldiers based in an army base at Mourmelon le Grand, a small town about 10 miles south west of Reims. Their mystery disappearances quickly led to an air of panic in the area — with people convinced a serial killer was on the loose.

The first to disappear was Patrick Dubois, who was a 19-year-old conscript. On January 4, 1980, he had been given an evening's leave from the base, where he was in the 4th Dragoon Regiment of the French Army, a cavalry unit.

When he failed to show up for his military duties the next morning, army authorities immediately suspected he had gone absent without leave — AWOL. He was described as shy and quiet and had only left home for the first time a few months earlier to begin his military service.

The only clue military police could find in relation to his whereabouts was that, on the evening he disappeared, he had written to his parents, mentioning that he was due to head to a local cinema at 8pm with another conscript. Police gave up looking for him after a few weeks and there has been no trace of him to this day.

More than a year later, on February 2, 1981, another young soldier vanished, Serge Havet, who was 20. He, like Dubois, was given a day's leave from his camp. His base was in the town of Mailly Le Camp, some 35 miles from Mourmelon, but on the same main road, the RN77.

He had only a few weeks left in military service and was in good form when he vanished. Friends said they had no doubt that his disappearance was involuntary. Like Dubois, he has never been found. And, like Dubois, he was accused in his absence of being a deserter.

Manuel Carvalho was the next to vanish. Like Dubois, Carvalho, who was 19, was based at the 4th Dragoon Regiment in Mourmelon. He was given a weekend pass from the base on August 7, 1981, and was never seen again.

Yet again, military authorities began an investigation based on the supposition that he was a deserter. He was a mechanic at the Mourmelon camp.

Less than three weeks later, another soldier vanished. This time it was a 20-yar-old conscript called Pascal Sergent, who was based with the 503rd Tank Regiment — again based at the sprawling Mourmelon base. He had been given a 72-hour pass and was last spotted hitch hiking on August 20.

His mother reported him missing on August 29. His family and friends said he loved the army and wanted to stay on after his period of mandatory military service was completed.

The disappearances stopped for more than a year after Sergent. But on October 1982 another soldier went missing.

Olivier Donner was also a member of the 4th Dragoon Regiment, based at Mourmelon. Like all the other cases, he vanished hours after being given leave.

But, unlike the other disappearances, it became apparent within weeks that cops were dealing with a murder. On October 30, just as military authorities began to search for Donner as a deserter, a hunter found his body dumped on the RN77, close to Mailly Le Camp.

The 20-year-old's body had been dumped in a small forest beside the main road. He was wearing the same clothes he had on when he left Mourmelon camp. His body was so badly decomposed that pathologists could not say how he died, or if he had been sexually assaulted. But they were satisfied he had been murdered.

The local police, the gendarmerie, began a murder inquiry and also started re-examining the other cases of the missing soldiers. But, within weeks, it became clear that they had no leads — and no suspects.

Gradually, the case was wound down and the media began to lose interest in the murder and the cases of the missing men.

But in August 1985, almost three years later, another young man vanished. On Friday, August 23, Patrice Denis (20) was dropped off by a colleague in Chalons-en-Champagne, a town 14 miles south of Mourmelon.

He was a civilian, but was heading to Mourmelon to take part in a science fair at the camp. He told his friend he would be hitch-hiking the rest of the way. He was never seen again.

The killer had, apparently, struck again. And this time it was a civilian. Police set up a massive investigation to try to find Denis and feared immediately he had been kidnapped. But there has been no trace of him.

The same fate befell another young man, again a soldier, in April 1987. The 19-year-old, called Patrick Gache, was based — like most of the others — at the 4th Dragoon Regiment in Mourmelon when he disappeared. And, like the others, he vanished as he made his way home to enjoy a few days leave. His body has never been recovered.

In just over seven years, seven young men had disappeared without a trace from a small area, no more than 35 miles wide, of north eastern France.

One body had been recovered, but cops by this stage feared the rest had been murdered and secretly buried.

They knew, by now, they were dealing with a serial killer who was vicious and was an expert at covering his tracks — and hiding bodies. There was an air of panic in the area when Gache disappeared. People were terrified.

They were worried that their brother or son could be next to disappear in what was now being dubbed the "triangle of death".

And it was into this triangle that a young Irishman walked, oblivious, in August 1987.

Trevor O'Keeffe (19) left his home in Naas, Co Kildare in late June 1987. He was a young man verging on adulthood and was off to Europe for an adventure, like so many people of his age.

His first step was to head to the UK. There he went to St Albans, a city in Hertfordshire, some 25 miles north-west of central London. He spent some time with his sister, Eroline, who was living in the town.

He worked as a barman in the city for several weeks, before he had another idea — a plan that would prove fatal for him. While he was working in the bar, he had become good friends with a Frenchman, called Christian.

He had told him he was heading back to France, and invited him to come with him. Trevor jumped at the chance and journeyed to Christian's home village of Poligny, in the foothills of the Alps and near the Swiss border in the south-east of the country.

He left the UK in the last week of July, arriving in France on August 1. He had planned to spend weeks, if not months, in Pologny, a village with a population of less than 300. But almost as soon as he got there, he knew there was a problem.

The village was simply too small for him to get a job. Worse, Christian's family was extremely poor — there was no way they could support him.

So, on August 2 — just two days after arriving in Poligny — he rang his sister Eroline in St Albans to say things weren't working out, and that he was on his way back to her.

He told Eroline that the journey would take him a few days, but he would be back to her soon. He set off the very next day.

He had his route planned with some precision. He intended to travel to Calais on the north-west coast of France, some 380 miles away. He wrote down on a piece of paper the route that he planned to take. He planned first to get to Dijon, then Troyes, then the town of Chalons en Champagne.

After that he would reach Reims, before heading to Saint

Quentin, then on to Calais and the ferry to Dover in England.

By car the journey is no more than seven hours and he decided to hitch-hike — what the French call autostop.

Back in the 1980s, hitching was hugely popular, especially with young people who simply did not have the money to take a train, plane or bus.

The practice is much less common nowadays, but back then many students hitched their way around Ireland and further afield. Trevor was used to hitching and had even put a tent and sleeping bag in his backpack, expecting the journey to take several days.

He set off early on the morning of August 3, 1987, and could reasonably have expected to be in the UK within two days.

Unbeknownst to him, the section of the journey from Troyes to Reims would take him right through France's grisly triangle of death — a place where seven young men had disappeared in the previous seven years. Mourmelon, the centre of the triangle, was just 15 miles north of the town of Chalons en Champagne.

Trevor was never seen alive again.

On August 8, five days after Trevor left Poligny heading towards Calais, farmer Michel Lente was walking on his land outside the small village of Alaincourt, close to Saint Quentin, a large town on the main road between Reims and Calais.

As he walked, the sharp-eyed farmer noticed something strange in a wooded area of his land. It was a long mound of earth that looked like it had been freshly dug. He moved closer. When he was a matter of feet away, he quickly realised something brutal and horrific had taken place on the land he cherished.

Now inches from the mound, he could see that it was a shallow grave. Inside the mound, he could clearly see the body of a young man, lying face down. He was fully clothed, apart from one shoe, which was missing.

There was a deep wound circling the young man's neck, and it was immediately apparent to the farmer that the victim had been strangled to death, before being given a hurried burial. Mr Lente also noticed that the victim's watch was still ticking as it sat on his wrist, which would later make French cops suspect the body had been left there a relatively short time ago.

Within minutes of the gruesome find the Gendarmes from Saint Quentin, some six miles north of Alaincourt, had been alerted and were on their way.

They carefully removed the body and began a search for clues in the area — they knew they were dealing with a murder and needed all the help they could get.

A few yards away, they found a white handkerchief, with the initials CHMP carefully embroidered in one of its corners.

They searched the body for clues to identification, but there was no identity card, passport or driving licence.

The cause looked pretty hopeless. But then, a sharp-eyed gendarme spotted something in the man's clothing. It was a small white business card from a business in St Albans. It was their only clue and they latched on to it.

By this stage, none of Trevor's family had heard from him, but were not unduly worried. This was 1987 and mobiles were practically unheard of — students and young people travelling abroad sent postcards or, at most, rang home once a week.

It was on August 12 that the family began to get concerned. That was Eroline's 22nd birthday. Trevor always rang her on her birthday. But not this year. The family began to think something had happened.

A few weeks later they got their answer.

One day, late in August, Eroline was in her office in St Albans when an English police officer walked in and asked to speak to her boss. He was out, so Eroline asked if she could help the detective.

What the officer said next changed not only Eroline's life for good, but the lives of the entire O'Keeffe family.

He explained that a young man's body had been found in France and the only clue was the business card from Eroline's company that had been found on the victim.

In an instant, Eroline knew that the body was Trevor's. She

had given him her boss's business card before he left. It could not be anyone else. Eroline informed her shocked family back in Ireland and her and Trevor's mother, also called Eroline, got the next flight from Dublin to Paris.

But it was too late. Six hours before she arrived in St Quentin, the French authorities had buried her beloved son in an unmarked, pauper's grave.

That was despite the fact that the police knew she was coming to take her son home, and had even booked a room in the local Hotel De Guise for her and her sister, Noeleen Slattery.

Ms O'Keeffe, who was a driving instructor in Naas, had the indignity of having to get lawyers involved to make sure Trevor could be exhumed and taken back to Ireland.

Amazingly, the judge who ordered the burial repeatedly refused to see them, despite their daily requests for a meeting. And, after a week of waiting in the hotel, they were told menacingly by local Gendarmes: "Go home now."

But they refused. And it was a full six weeks before the decision was made to allow Trevor's body to be exhumed.

Eroline was present when the grave was opened. The grave-diggers used a mechanical digger to lift the coffin out of the hole. And then disaster. The coffin was lifted out clumsily and it fell to earth. It broke open and Trevor's corpse, wrapped in plastic, fell out in front of his mother. The two women were enveloped in a foul stench — and surrounded by a horde of flies. Eroline then had to go and buy two coffins, one lead lined — for her son's final journey home.

But the humiliation did not end there.

Several months after Trevor's murder, a letter arrived at Eroline's home, addressed to her dead son. It had a French postmark. When Eroline opened, she was amazed and horrified by its contents.

The letter was written by a lady called Joelle Charnel. She had found Trevor's haversack and documentation when she was walking on land close to her home in Droyes, 25 miles south of where Trevor's body had been buried.

She made the discovery of his haversack, birth certificate and his registration document for the FCA, the precursor of today's Reserve Defence Forces, which contained his address.

She first went to her local police station, but they were uninterested and told her to keep the items in her garage until someone came for them.

But Ms Charnel was worried about the young man whose possessions she had found and decided to write to him, asking if he was ok. Eroline would later say that Ms Charnel was not only more efficient than the local police — but more humane.

These affronts to the family by the French judicial system were only the first in a litany of horrors that would last another 16 years.

While Eroline was trying to come to terms with her son's murder, not to mention the disgraceful way the French had treated her, the authorities were beginning a murder hunt.

Right from the start, they suspected a soldier, or someone with military training, had been involved in Trevor's murder. Trevor had been strangled to death with a garrotte. That is a piece of material used by military units to kill a sentry from a hostile force, silently and quickly.

The soldier creeps up on his target from behind and wraps the wire or piece of cord around the enemy's neck, holding it tight until he dies. It takes less than a minute and the subject can't even scream for help.

The garrotte found on Trevor's body was identical to that used by the French military. It was specially knotted, in a way only the French military tied theirs.

Mourmelon, where the seven young men had disappeared in the previous seven years, was less than half an hour away. It didn't take a genius to work out that Trevor's death was probably linked to their disappearances — and that the likely culprit was probably a soldier based at the sprawling Mour-melon camp.

But, even though the murder of an Irish tourist was major news in the area and in France as a whole, the investigation petered out after a few months. There was no suspect. The cops did not have a clue.

All that changed, however, exactly one year and a day after Trevor's body was found.

On August 9, 1988, two gendarmes were on patrol in an isolated area of Macon, some 250 miles south-west of Mourmelon. They saw a Vokswagen camper van parked on a lonely path. The officers, suspicious, approached and knocked on the window. A soldier rolled down the window. The offi-cers asked him for his identity cards and his name.

"Pierre Chanal," he said, handing over his papers. The cops were just about to leave when one of them looked in to the back of the vehicle.

He could not believe the sight that greeted him. A young man lay faced down under a blanket, trussed up in such a way that he would strangle himself if he moved. The man, who was foreign, spoke no French but managed to gesture to the cops that he was in serious trouble. He mimed that Chanal had kidnapped and sexually assaulted him.

Chanal, a strapping soldier, told the cops that the man was gay and that they were lovers. The gendarmes looked at the Hungarian, then looked back at Chanal.

He was a warrant officer, or sergeant major, in the French army. He looked totally respectable. They almost believed him, but decided to give the foreigner the benefit of the doubt and arrested Chanal on suspicion of rape and kidnapping.

However, as they led Chanal away, they warned the dishevelled victim: "You are in trouble if you are lying."

Chanal, who was based at Fontainebleu, south of Paris, but before that had spent most of his military career in Mourmel-on, stuck to the military script.

Trained in anti-interrogation techniques, he would only tell the cops his name, rank and serial number.

The victim, however, was much more forthcoming.

He told cops that he was Hungarian and his name was Palasz Falvay. He had just turned 20 and had spent the last month hitch-hiking around France when hell came to him in a camper van.

He told officers that he was hitch-hiking near Chalon — 40 miles west of Poligny where Trevor was last seen on August 6. A man in a Volkswagen stopped for him at around 10pm and agreed to take him south, to Lyon.

After about 40 miles, the driver pulled into a quiet area in Macon. He pretended that he was lost and got into the back of the van, as if looking for something.

Suddenly, Mr Falvay said, the man came at him from behind, put a khaki strap around his neck and gripped it tight.

"He was like a madman," he recalled. "He was excited, his eyes were bulging. I was afraid that he was going to kill me."

The man then repeatedly sexually assaulted him over a period of several hours. When dawn came, Chanal realised that cars were close by, so he moved off again.

He stopped once he reached a quiet spot and raped Mr Falvay two or three times. He also produced a video camera and made Mr Falvay touch himself.

"I don't know what his plan was to do to me and I can't bear to think what might have happened to me if your colleagues had not arrived," he told the French police. "In my opinion, he was really capable of doing the worst. He was really mad, very nervous, on the edge of hysteria. I tell you this, I was terrified."

Within months, Chanal (42) went on trial for the rape, abduction and sexual assault of Mr Falvay.

Cops would later carry out an investigation into Chanal's background and realise he had endured a nightmare childhood of poverty and abuse.

He was one of 17 children on the family farm living in fear of their violent father, who regularly attacked their mother.

Chanal often tried to break up fights between the couple but was in turn beaten up by his father. The children slept in two small rooms on the rented farm where the family suffered grinding poverty.

Chanal left school at 14 and became an apprentice baker before joining the army four years later. There, he found happiness. The strict regime, the physical exertion every day, the discipline and camaraderie all suited him. He was regarded as a top soldier, much respected by officers and soldiers alike.

But that stood for nothing when he appeared in court in 1990, charged with rape and kidnapping.

Mr Falvay came from Hungary to give evidence and face down Chanal, the man who was within minutes of killing him, were it not for the fortuitous appearance of the French officers that August night.

Chanal pleaded not guilty and took to the stand himself, where he gave sickening evidence on his night of pleasure with Mr Falvay — and claimed the sex was consensual.

"The young man wore really tight-fitting shorts and was roller skating. He got into my van voluntarily," he insisted. "He did not consent at the start, but as the night went on he agreed."

Mr Falvay's version, however, was diametrically opposed to what Chanal had claimed.

"I had to obey him to survive," he told the court in Chalons sur Saone. "If I did not do that, he would undoubtedly have killed me. At one stage I thought about killing him. There was a knife in the van, but I could not reach it."

And chillingly, he added: "I got the impression that I was not the first victim in the van, with all the instruments, chains and sex toys I saw inside."

Chanal was later convicted and jailed for 10 years.

But, in the meantime, other information had emerged that convinced the French press that Chanal was a serial killer — the man behind the disappearances in the triangle of death around Mourmelon.

Investigations revealed that Chanal had been based in Mourmelon from 1980 to 1986 — the time of most of the disappearances. From 1986 until August 1988, he was based at

Fontainebleau — but returned to Mourmelon every weekend to practise parachuting.

The only time he was constantly away from Mourmelon was for six months between 1985 and 1986, when he was on UN peacekeeping duty in Lebanon.

There were no disappearances in Mourmelon during his tour of duty with the French forces in Beirut.

A trove of disturbing evidence had also been found in Chanal's van that not only suggested strongly he had been involved in Trevor O'Keeffe's death — but also other men.

Cops who searched the camper van found 33 pairs of men's underpants. One of the pairs was size 30, Trevor's size, and said on it "Made in England". When Trevor had been found, he was wearing size 40 underpants — far too big for him — that were French made.

There were also dozens of different specimens of human hairs found in the van.

And this is where the French police began to mess up the investigation.

Eroline, Trevor's mother, had by now become aware of Chanal and had strong suspicions that he had killed her son.

When Trevor's body had been found, he was wearing white socks with stripes right at the top. An identical pair was found in Chanal's van — but the police said it was merely a coincidence.

Ms O'Keeffe then formally identified the UK-made underpants also found in Chanal's van as being Trevor's. But, again, the police said it was a coincidence.

The handkerchief that had been found close to Trevor's body bore the initials CHPM, which match Chanal's full name, Chanal Pierre Marcel. Again, the police said it was a coincidence.

Then, it emerged that soil on a spade found in the van was a complete match for the earth in which Trevor had been buried after his murder. But, once more, the French police said it was nothing more than a coincidence.

With no leads, Trevor's file lay dormant, the case unsolved

for years.

It was only in 1993 — six years after Trevor's murder — that the tide began to change.

French police began to reassess the evidence, after protests from Ms O'Keeffe and the families of the seven other men — six of whose bodies were never found.

Under enormous pressure, the French police used new scientific techniques to examine a large number of hairs found in Chanal's van. Using relatively new laser analysis officers satisfied themselves that one of the hairs definitely belonged to Patrick Gache, who disappeared in April 1987 — months before Trevor was killed. Tests were also carried out to examine the other hairs found in the van, but were inconclusive.

And an elderly lady who lived near Mourmelon came forward to claim that she had seen Chanal on many occasions as he parked his Volkswagen camper van close to her home — with young men inside each time.

She also said she used to hear screams from the van and on one occasion had even found bloodstains where it had been parked.

The families' campaign, the lady's statement, the breakthrough on the Gache inquiry all combined in late 1994 — seven years after Trevor's death — to persuade the French authorities to move against Chanal.

In November of that year, he was told he was being what the French call 'mis en examen' for the murder of Trevor and the seven other men — even though only two bodies had been found. Being a 'mis en examen' is effectively the same as being charged in Ireland or Britain, although it means the investigation is still under way and no prosecution takes place at this stage.

Chanal, by now locked up in a prison, reacted furiously to the news. The very next day, on November 16, Chanal tried to kill himself by slitting his wrists. But his bid to avoid facing justice for the eight men's deaths was doomed to failure — the wounds were only superficial and he survived.

A month later came news that nobody, not even Chanal,

was expecting. The investigating judge in the case — who under French law oversees police investigations and decides on what charges suspects should face — declared that Chanal would soon be a free man. And, despite being charged with the murders of eight men, Chanal was due to walk free from prison in mid 1995, when he had served his sentence for the kidnap and rape of Mr Falvay.

Chanal walked free from prison in July of 1995 after an appeal against his release was refused by a judge.

Hours earlier, Ms O'Keeffe had stood in the same court and identified the English-made underpants found in Chanal's van as belonging to Trevor.

She could simply not believe he was being released and began to have suspicions that there were greater influences at play in the Chanal case.

"Chanal has been protected by the French system because he is military," she said.

By this stage, Ms O'Keeffe was beginning to realise how slowly the wheels of French justice turned.

Even though DNA technology had been in widespread use in France since the late 1980s, shortly after Trevor's murder, it was not until 1996, that experts turned to it in relation to the Chanal case.

They asked close relatives of all the missing and murdered men, including Ms O'Keeffe, to provide a DNA sample.

They asked for this so they could compare those samples to the different types of human hair found in Chanal's van.

Incredibly, Mrs O'Keeffe and the others would have to wait more than three years for the results. They showed, conclusively, that some of the hair in the van was Trevor's — he had been in the vehicle.

The hair of two of the missing young men were also matched to two of the Frenchmen, Patrick Gache and Patrick Denis.

Tests on the other five missing men were inconclusive. Other tests had also been carried out on the mud found on the shovel in Chanal's car and that matched 100 per cent the earth where Trevor's body was found.

There was now more than enough evidence against Chanal and he was told that he was to be formally prosecuted for the three men's murders.

It had taken 12 years but, finally, the French had moved against Trevor's killer.

All Ms O'Keeffe had to do now was to hold out for the trial.

It would be a long wait, however.

The O'Keeffes had to wait another four years before the trial was scheduled to take place — even though he had been on bail since 1995 for the crimes.

In May of that year, the first attempt at a trial had to be aborted when Chanal, who was by now 56, took an overdose of sleeping pills.

Again, he survived that suicide bid and the trial was only put back for several days. But, bizarrely, the night before it was due to begin again, Chanal suffered a blood clot on his lungs. He was rushed to intensive care and was placed on a respirator.

This time the trial judge decided Chanal could not face justice in his present state and adjourned the case for several months. That decision enraged Ms O'Keeffe and members of the other victims' families.

Several of the French families shouted at the judge, demanding justice immediately. Ms O'Keeffe was more measured, but launched a withering attack on Chanal.

"It is a scam," she said. "He is putting on an act. It is a scam by him to keep him from the trial."

Despite the protests, the judge ruled the case would be held five months later in October.

Almost immediately after his suicide bid, Chanal tried another tactic in his bid to cheat justice: he went on a hunger strike. By October, days before the trial started, his lawyer claimed he had lost almost eight stone, now weighing in at only seven stone. The prison authorities, however, said they were checking him and said he weighed a healthy 10 stone.

This time there would be no delay. On October 14, Eroline

O'Keeffe, her sister Noeleen Slattery and her children Eroline, James and Julia sat in a front row of the assize court in Reims as judge Christine Simon-Rosenthal opened the case against Chanal.

The families of the two other victims, as well as the missing men, also packed into the courtroom — but one chair was empty. The space reserved for Chanal was unoccupied,

He had refused to leave prison for the case, and the judge decided it would go ahead in his absence.

The first day's hearing lasted only a few hours, with no major evidence heard against Chanal. Although prosecutors did say there was a mass of proof to show that Chanal had killed the three men, including DNA evidence that they had all been in his camper van, the stage was set for a trial lasting several weeks.

Several hours after the court ended for the day, two legal clerks were sent to Chanal's hospital prison cell to brief him on the day's events. He said nothing as the two men filled him in.

They left the cell at 11pm. At 11.30pm, midnight and 12.30am, a police officer checked on Chanal, who was deemed a high risk because of his previous suicide attempts.

On each occasion that the officer checked on him, Chanal was fine. But, at 12.38am, an officer checked on him again and became suspicious. He rushed in to the cell and found Chanal unconscious in a pool of blood.

He had used a commando technique to try to take his own life. Someone had smuggled in two blades for him and he had cut the arteries in each of his thighs.

He had even used elastic from his trousers to form two tourniquets, which he wrapped around each thigh, to ensure he would bleed to death even more quickly.

The officer immediately called a doctor who, one minute later, pronounced Pierre Marcel Chanal dead.

The beast of Mourmelon, the man who brought so much pain to countless men and their families, had cheated justice.

He had bled to death in around seven minutes. The next day,

the families were gathered in the courtroom waiting for the trial proper to begin when the news was broken to them.

Eroline O'Keeffe, a mother who had campaigned so long for justice for her son, was distraught — and felt that she had been cheated of justice.

"We didn't strive for Chanal's suicide," she said outside the court. "We strove for truth and justice, and he robbed us of that, just as he robbed me of my son."

And she said she felt French authorities wanted Chanal dead. "They allowed it to happen By taking his own life, Mr Chanal ensured that legally he will be forever presumed innocent, despite damning evidence. I think his suicide proves his guilt," she said.

The lawyer for the French victims agreed. Gerard Chemla surveyed the scene outside the court and simply said: "Pierre Chanal has gone away with his secrets. He has committed his last crime."

No young men disappeared around Mourmelon when Chanal was in jail. And no young men vanished in the area after he killed himself. It's clear now that the beast of Mourmelon was Pierre Chanal, a highly respected soldier — but a man who had a gruesome secret.

Ms O'Keeffe was so incensed by the French handling of the case that she immediately sued the authorities for alleged negligence. The other families later joined her in the case.

Almost two years later, Eroline O'Keeffe sat in the cafe, a few yards from Paris' Palais de Justice as justice of a kind was handed down to her.

The €25,000 she was awarded in settlement of the case would never bring Trevor back. It wouldn't even cover her expenses. But it gave her something much more important.

Vindication for her son.

PHOEBE PRINCE:
Schoolgirl bullied to her death

PHOEBE Prince looked out across the vast Atlantic. It was her last day in Ireland and she was filled with excitement at the adventure that lay ahead.

The fifteen-year-old was about to embark on a life-changing journey that would see her leave behind the sleepy village of Fanore in Co Clare and move to the United States.

A new start in America was supposed to bring with it all the traditional promise of opportunity and life. Her mother, Anne O'Brien Prince, had family on the east coast. Along with Phoebe's father, she had decided that it would be a once-in-a-lifetime chance for her two youngest daughters to broaden their horizons.

But as her father Jeremy now admits, it was an experiment that went disastrously wrong .

Phoebe arrived in South Hadley in Massachusetts with her mother Anne and her younger sister Lauren in September 2009. Jeremy and three other siblings stayed behind in Ireland while his wife and two youngest daughters gave living in America a trial run. If everything went to plan the rest of family would consider relocating.

They could not have imagined that, just five months later, Phoebe's lifeless body would be found hanging in her wardrobe — the last desperate act of teenager whose very existence had been made a living hell by a gang of bullies.

This shocking turn of events was as far away from the American dream as possible and the death of Phoebe Prince made major news in America and beyond. Six teenagers would face charges including statutory rape, in relation to her death. It was a tragedy which plunged the US into an episode of soul-searching not seen since the Columbine school massacre.

With its population of almost 20,000 people, its low crime rate and its tidy clapboard houses behind miles of white picket fences, South Hadley is one of several middle-class towns that line the Connecticut River valley about 90 miles from Boston. It is the picture postcard America, a sleepy town that cherishes sport and family values and espouses the American way.

For Phoebe, enrolling in South Hadley High School was exciting but also nerve-wracking. The school is a sports-mad institution and a springboard for America's Ivy League system. Would the girl from rural Ireland fit it? What would her peers make of the newcomer, a pretty brunette with sparkling eyes, a love for fashion and a sharp, inquisitive mind?

The Irish-born human rights academic and Obama advisor Samantha Power once said that her experience going from an Irish secondary school into the clique-ish "jockocracy" of an American high school had prepared her like nothing else for work in the world's most dangerous war zones.

Phoebe probably took some comfort from South Hadley's strong Irish heritage. There is a large Irish immigrant community in western Massachusetts dating from the refugees who fled the famine of the 1840s, and the region remains one of the most heavily Irish areas of the country. In South Hadley, 16 per cent of the population are of Irish descent.

After arriving in the new town, Phoebe's mother quickly rented a picket fence-fronted duplex on Newton Street, a few blocks from South Hadley High School. A few weeks after she arrived, Phoebe told her friends back in Ireland that being in America was like living in a movie.

At school, her new classmates regarded her as something of a novelty when she arrived in their midst, the majority interested to know more about her. Life, at first, was good — Phoebe made friends and later developed a crush on a fellow student, Sean Mulveyhill.

As the 17-year-old captain of the school's football team and a senior, Mulveyhill was the quintessential American high-school heart-throb. Indeed, in a recent South Hadley High yearbook he had been given the title 'classroom flirt'.

So when Sean in turn took notice of the pretty new girl with her lilting Irish accent, Phoebe was on cloud nine.

In October, freshman Phoebe and Sean went on a date. Things quickly turned serious and they had sex. But the relationship didn't last and in November, Sean broke up with Phoebe and began seeing his hockey champion ex-girlfriend again, childhood sweetheart Kayla Narey (17).

Though broken-hearted in the way that only a teenager can be, Phoebe may have believed her brief relationship with Sean might open up doors for her and allow her befriend some of the more popular students. But in dating the captain of the football team, she had unwittingly stirred a hornets' nest of resentment among the so-called mean girls of the school, who were horrified that the "new girl" had snared one of their most prized assets.

This was Phoebe's first and only mistake — and she was soon singled out for a vicious campaign of bullying.

The pretty brunette was targeted on multiple fronts — she was openly and persistently abused in school, labelled an "Irish slut", and physically attacked. The abuse never let up — and it spread through technology, resulting in Phoebe's suffering extending far past the gates of South Hadley High.

Her phone number was circulated and she received countless abusive text messages. Facebook, the social-networking site that has transformed the lives of students, was quickly adopted as a means by which to ridicule her.

One student, Ashlee Dunn (16), later told the *New York Times* she had heard stories spread about Phoebe in the hallways. "She was new and she was from a different country and she didn't really know the school very well," Ashlee recalled. "I think that's probably one reason why they chose Phoebe."

Phoebe's tormentors were a group of popular, attractive girls dubbed the 'mean girls', a name taken from the 2004 movie of the same name. Starring Lindsay Lohan, the comic movie told the story of a student who took on the popular girls and won. But for Phoebe there would be no such victory.

As Kevin Cullen of the *Boston Globe* put it, these girls decided "that Phoebe didn't know her place and that Phoebe would pay".

So began a three-month campaign of mental and sometimes physical torture by Kayla Narey, Sean Mulveyhill and his 16-year-old friend Ashley Longe against Phoebe.

Soon after her break-up with Mulveyhill, Phoebe attempted to take her own life by swallowing a bottle of pills. Unbeknownst to her tormentors, the Irish schoolgirl had a history of depression and self-harming and had been prescribed anti-depression medications in the past.

As Phoebe recovered from her overdose attempt, her father Jeremy visited. Phoebe was encouraged to see a therapist, who provided her parents with a letter stating she was not a suicide risk. Her worried parents accepted the overdose was a "call for help" and set about trying to help her settle in.

A week later Phoebe bravely returned to school and, in what can only have been a desperate bid to escape the attentions of her tormentors, she had a second, brief encounter with an 18-year-old boy called Austin Renaud. But far from easing her anguish this only led to even more pain for Phoebe — as Renaud's 16-year-old former girlfriend Flannery Mullins and her 16-year-old friend Sharon Chanon Velazquez then began a campaign of their own against Phoebe.

Schoolgirl bullied to her death

In court documents, Mullins is recorded as saying she was going to "beat Phoebe up" and also told her to "watch out." Longe, meanwhile, publicly harassed Phoebe, telling her to "close her legs" and screaming that she "hated stupid sluts".

The bullying was having a dire effect and Phoebe repeatedly arrived late for classes, in tears. Around this time, a teacher was seen comforting her while she wept in a corridor. But on a different occasion, two other teachers are said to have watched and done nothing as bullies hurled abuse at her in the school canteen.

Christmas 2009 must have brought some mild relief for Phoebe. Her father Jeremy was still with the family and, as school closed for a few weeks, Phoebe's thoughts were full of Ireland and her friends at home.

Her childhood in west Clare was about as far away from her new life as she could ever imagine. Phoebe grew up in tiny Ardeamish, which nestles on the Co Clare coast between Doolin and Lisdoonvarna. Her family arrived there from Bedford in England, in 1996, when Phoebe was just two.

Her father Jeremy Prince had come to work as a landscape gardener, selling blueberries, shrubs and other plants. Her mother Anne O'Brien had gone back to college later in life. She had qualified as a schoolteacher and had taken up a post at the local Mary Immaculate Secondary School.

Phoebe's younger sister Lauren was a keen athlete, and along with her three older siblings Simon, Tessa and Bridget the family prospered in Co Clare. For most of their lives the Prince children lived with their parents in a picturesque house at the back of the cemetery, facing the wild Atlantic ocean.

The Princes were well liked and are described by locals as "very decent people". Jeremy would regularly drop into the local pub and Phoebe was extremely close to him.

On an online blog set up by one of her English teachers, she described the long chats they had: "No subject is off limits... sex, drugs and rock and roll to ancient religions, politics and criminal justice." The Princes were a close family, blessed with loving parents.

At home in Ireland, Phoebe went to school in the exclusive Villiers college in nearby Limerick, where she is remembered as a warm, outgoing girl popular in a coed boarding school environment where friends were made for life. Villiers is a fee-paying school and the student body is diverse and multi-denominational.

It is a nursery for many distinguished former pupils including politician Jan O'Sullivan, and prides itself on its reputation as a nurturing environment. Phoebe thrived there.

Returning to her new school after the Christmas holidays, perhaps Phoebe had decided that one year might be enough in America. She would complete her 12 months and then return home to her family, to her friends, to a country she knew and understood.

But Phoebe Prince would not see out the bitter winter storms of January.

Back in South Hadley High, the bullying was as bad as ever. Friends said Phoebe was shoved into lockers and encouraged to kill herself on Facebook. In the first weeks of January, Phoebe's frame of mind worsened. In a class essay she wrote about self mutilation, sending a clear signal to her teachers that all was not well.

One essay written by Phoebe was a review of a book called Cutting by Dr Steven Levenkron, an expert on anorexia nervosa. In her review Phoebe wrote: "From a personal point of view I can see that Levenkron does truly understand the concept of self-mutilation and how it's not about suicide, in most cases it's about trying to transfer the pain from emotional to physical pain which is a lot easier to deal with for most adolescents who most likely don't even understand how they're feeling."

Schoolgirl bullied to her death

Self-harm is a well known warning sign that someone may be at risk of taking their own life. In another essay Phoebe wrote that she disliked Facebook and Twitter — hardly surprising given that she was being mercilessly bullied online.

Three days before Phoebe's death, a student confided in a staff member that someone had scratched Phoebe's face out of a class photo and drawn something obscene over it. The teacher later took the picture down, but further damage had been done.

"Phoebe had to go into that classroom and see that on one of the last days of her life," the mother of a fellow student subsequently told a local newspaper. The woman would only speak on the condition of anonymity as she feared her own daughter might suffer a backlash.

On the night of January 13, Phoebe had a telephone conversation with an older female friend about what she was going to wear to the cotillion, the school dance that was held two days later. She had chosen a short, black lace dress. "I saw it. It was pretty," the woman, who has declined to be named, said. "We had a long debate about whether she should wear red or pink shoes, whether she should wear [tights] or not. She loved fashion. She seemed cheerful."

Less than 24 hours later Phoebe was dead.

On the morning of January 14 Phoebe walked to school as normal. But according to court documents, not long after arriving she told school officials that she was "scared and wanted to go home". When the school refused to allow this, Phoebe went back to class and told a classmate that she expected to be beaten up that day.

After class she visited the nurses office and was seen crying hysterically. At lunchtime friends said Phoebe tried to find solace in her iPod, about which she had once written: "I have a song for every moment and mood of my day."

Later in the day, Phoebe went to the library with friends. There at the same time were Kayla Narey, Sean Mulveyhill, and Ashley Longe. According to prosecutors, Longe began yelling "I hate stupid sluts" and other sexual slurs at Phoebe.

She later called Phoebe an "Irish whore" and wrote similar descriptions on the library sign-in sheets.

At the end of the school day, Longe allegedly again screamed "Why don't you just open your legs?" at Phoebe in the school auditorium. Mulveyhill encouraged Longe's behaviour and also called Phoebe a "whore", while Narey, sitting nearby, was allegedly laughing. The abuse continued even once the school day had ended as Longe threw an empty sports drink can from a car at Phoebe, who was walking home. Longe laughed and called her a whore, court documents say. Phoebe, according to witnesses, was crying.

A friend of Phoebe's, Sergio Loubriel, revealed how he had made plans with Phoebe for that evening. She planned to call to his house after her dinner.

"In the hallways, people would give little smart remarks, just look at her funny like she had three eyes," Loubriel later said. He added that students called her a "slut" and an "Irish whore," but Phoebe, he said, never discussed her worries with him. "Right away they just jumped on her without even giving her a try," Loubriel said.

That evening, Phoebe never showed up to their arranged meeting. Sergio would never see his friend again.

Phoebe had walked the rest of the journey home in tears and went straight into her bedroom where she sent a last text message to a close male friend.

"I cant do it anymore," she wrote. "im literally hme cryn, my scar on my chest is potentially permanent, my bodies fukd up what mre do they want frm me? Du I hav to fukn od!"

Phoebe plugged her mobile phone into a charger, presumably to provide investigators with evidence of her torment. Then she went into a closet and hanged herself with a scarf her younger sister had bought her for Christmas.

The horrific discovery of Phoebe's body was made by her 12-year-old sister Lauren, who immediately rang 911. By

4.40pm the house was surrounded by police and paramedics but they were unable to revive Phoebe.

Within hours the tragic news had spread like wildfire through South Hadley. Flowers were scattered outside the house, candles were lit and a group of neighbours hovered near the white picket fence outside the house. That night, in the car park of the school, a group of students held a candlelit vigil. Friends helped a distraught Anne O'Brien to pack up her belongings and move to her sister's. She would never again live in the house on Newton Street.

Far from being contrite about their systematic campaign of harassment, Phoebe's tormentors continued with their sick antics even after her death. Indications of the extreme levels of cruelty these bullies were capable of was evident from the malicious messages posted on a Facebook tribute page set up after her death. A few hours after Phoebe's death a one-word message appeared: "Accomplished." Other comments were also posted online stating Phoebe had gotten what she deserved.

Two days after Phoebe's death, the local 'Cotillion' dance she had been due to attend went ahead. Despite the fact that one of their own had died, some 500 students of South Hadley attended the dance.

One girl, Katie Broderick, who would later speak on camera to reporters about her shock and upset at Phoebe's death, was pictured laughing at the Cotillion with the boy who had gone out with Phoebe, Sean Mulveyhill. Mulveyhill himself posted pictures of the event on his Facebook page. It was later revealed by popular US TV psychologist Dr Phil McGraw that some students even mimicked the hanging of Phoebe at the dance.

At a service two days later, wearing the dress she had chosen to wear to the dance, Phoebe's body was laid out at St Patrick's Catholic Church in South Hadley. As Somewhere Over The Rainbow was played, many of those gathered wept openly. There was a contingent of people from Clare, including many of Phoebe's family.

In the following days a death notice appeared in the paper in which her grieving relatives wrote: "Phoebe was gifted with exceptional beauty — but that is not important. She was gifted with a sharp and creative brain — but that is not important. She had impressive artistic talent — but that is not important.

"What her family and friends from both sides of the Atlantic grieve is the loss of the incandescent enthusiasm of a life blossoming."

They revealed that they had set up a scholarship fund in Phoebe's name. The notice ended with a quote in Irish: "Go gcoinni Dia i mbois a laimhe thu" — 'May God keep you in the palm of his hand'.

Phoebe would later be cremated and her ashes brought back to Ireland, where a service was held for her at a packed church in Fanore, Co Clare.

Initially, Phoebe's death was classed as another teen suicide by the authorities — a tragically regular occurrence in US public schools. South Hadley police chief David LaBrie said: "A teenage girl appears to have taken her own life ... a myriad of issues could have been involved." Gus Sayer, the superintendent for South Hadley High, revealed Phoebe had been having counselling for "adjustment issues" but said he could not speculate on why she did what she did.

However, Phoebe's classmates were perfectly prepared to voice their own theories. The names of the four girls alleged to be involved in bullying Phoebe were buzzing all over the internet by that weekend. A Facebook page was set up entitled "Expel the Girls Who Caused Phoebe Prince To Commit Suicide". It soon had over 20,000 members, including Phoebe's brother Simon and several of her friends. Another Facebook page entitled "We Murdered Phoebe Prince" listed the names of the girls and had to be removed by the website.

Online, where Phoebe had endured so much harassment, the war of words over her death intensified. The addresses and phone numbers of the four girls alleged to have been involved in bullying Phoebe were posted on several web forums. One of the bullies responded with extreme callousness. A screenshot of a Facebook post (since removed) by one of the girls alleged to have been involved reads: "It was her own fault." This same girl later joined remembrance and anti-bullying groups online.

A few days after Phoebe's death, school authorities and local police confirmed they were investigating the young girl's death amid claims she was the victim of a vicious bullying campaign. The national media took an interest — and a story began to emerge of a school in the grip of a bullying pandemic.

When one TV station sent a crew to South Hadley High to interview pupils, one girl spoke out on camera about the bullying that was endemic in the school. Once the TV crew was out of sight, one of Phoebe's tormentors reportedly came up and slammed the girl who had been interviewed against a locker and punched her in the head.

As grief and anger over Phoebe's tragic death grew, the management of South Hadley High came under pressure. Parents wanted to know how a child could be so badly bullied that she would resort to ending her own life — and why her teachers had not been able to put a stop to her ordeal.

In a letter to parents days after Phoebe's suicide, principal Daniel Smith responded by saying: "Some students made mean-spirited comments to Phoebe in school and on the way home from school but also through texting and social networking websites. This insidious, harassing behaviour knows no bounds." He said the school was convening a task force to try and develop constructive ways to address bullying and confirmed that a few students had come forward, saying that Phoebe was bullied because of dating issues.

"Phoebe was a smart, charming — and as is the case with many teenagers — complicated young person who truly valued her close friends and her family," he wrote. "We will never know the specific reasons why she chose to take her life.

However, both local and state police investigations are looking into the role that bullying may have played in her decision.

"Now that we've had a chance to console our student body and we've begun the grieving as a school community, we too, will conduct an investigation to try to ascertain to what degree school-related bullying may have played a role in Phoebe's decision," said Mr Smith, who has since retired from his post.

South Hadley Superintendent Gus Sayer released a statement in late January saying he was aware of the bullying claims, adding that it was a subject the school had taken seriously even before the Co Clare girl's death. He said the school had, in recent years implemented policies on bullying and run programmes to alert students to the nature of the problem. Two students, he also confirmed, had been disciplined a few weeks before Prince's death, but no details were given to state what the discipline consisted of. The breach of conduct had apparently involved the student bursting into Phoebe's class and screaming insults at her.

But as the school authorities tried to keep a handle on the situation, fresh examples of bullying continued to seep out. One student told local reporters that other children had moved from the town because they could not deal with the bullying. Former student Lex Zypher described South Hadley High's car park as a "war zone." Dozens of commentators on a Massachusetts news site also claimed it was well-known in the town who was carrying out the bullying which led to Phoebe's death. South Hadley High, it appeared, had had a long-standing and very serious problem with bullying.

It emerged that in the very month Phoebe arrived in the town, school authorities had decided that things were so out of hand that they arranged for Barbara Colloroso, a nationally renowned expert on bullying, to pay a visit. Colloroso had previously been brought in to the Red Lake reservation in Minnesota after a 16-year-old shot dead seven people at the school where he had been bullied.

Colloroso duly emphasised that unchecked bullying could result in suicides, copy-cat suicides, dropping out of or transferring out of school and tragedies like the Columbine High School shootings. A teacher and 12 students were shot dead in the Colorado school in 1999 by two gun-wielding students who had been ridiculed as being homosexuals.

In terms of South Hadley, Colloroso said one of the biggest problems was that the school had no clear policy on cyberbullying. But on the day of her seminar only 10 parents showed up. South Hadley High may have known it had a problem, but when it came to solving it, the desire to act was sorely lacking.

In the weeks after Phoebe's death, Ms Colloroso came forward and said the schoolgirl had been called "an Irish slut" and this constituted an ethnic and sexual slur and, as such, was a hate crime. She also lambasted school officials for letting the perpetrators remain in school while being investigated.

Towards the end of January, less than two weeks after Phoebe's death, hundreds of South Hadley High School graduates, students and parents attended a school committee meeting to share their experiences of bullying. Regret was voiced that a young girl who came to seek out the American dream had been returned to her shores for burial. Action was demanded. The parents of South Hadley wanted heads to roll.

In mid-February there was a public meeting at which passions ran high. Hundreds of parents called for those who had been involved in "driving this girl to kill herself" to be removed from the school. They had collected over 1,000 signatures for a petition demanding action on the part of the school board.

On February 22, South Hadley Superintendent Gus Sayer announced that a number of the girls who bullied Phoebe would not be re-enrolling at South Hadley High. He declined to comment on whether the students had left voluntarily before they could be expelled. Principal Daniel Smith added: "These students' lives have also been dramatically altered ... They won't be graduating from South Hadley High School."

More important, however, was the announcement that the Northeastern District Attorney, Elizabeth Scheibel, was looking into the case. While Phoebe Prince's death may have caused a storm, the actions of this no-nonsense DA would create a tsunami.

After a two-and-a-half month criminal probe, Scheibel convened a press conference and began by saying that the abuse dished out to Phoebe — online and in person — was far greater than had previously been reported. Scheibel said that the suspects' "relentless activity directed toward Phoebe was designed to humiliate her and to make it impossible for her to remain at school". She added: "Their conduct far exceeded the limits of normal teenage relationship-related quarrels." Phoebe, she said, took her own life after a torturous day during which she was subjected to verbal harassment and threatened with physical abuse.

Scheibel told the packed audience that six students in South Hadley, where 16 is the legal age of adulthood, would face charges in relation to her death — including two who were charged with statutory rape.

Phoebe's ex-boyfriend Sean Mulveyhill, who so callously abandoned her after their short-lived affair, was indicted on four charges — statutory rape, violation of civil rights with bodily injury, criminal harassment and disturbance of school assembly.

And 18-year-old Austin Renaud, who also had sex with Phoebe, was also charged with statutory rape.

Sean's on-off girlfriend Kayla Narey was charged with violation of civil rights with bodily injury, criminal harassment and disturbance of school assembly.

Ashley Longe was charged with violation of civil rights with bodily injury as a youthful offender.

Flannery Mullins (16), who took an intense dislike to Phoebe after she slept with her former boyfriend Austin Renaud, was charged with violation of civil rights with bodily injury and stalking as a youthful offender.

Schoolgirl bullied to her death

Sharon Velazquez (16) was hit with a charge of violation of civil rights with bodily injury and stalking as a youthful offender.

In a carefully-worded statement, Scheibel also dropped another bombshell. She stated that school officials knew about the bullying, but added none would face criminal charges.

The reaction to the charges divided the town as the reality of what faced the students hit home. Statutory rape charges can result in penalties of up to life in prison, while conviction on a violation of civil rights charge could result in a 10-year jail sentence.

For the most part, the families of the accused withdrew from the limelight, all refusing to comment except the mother of Sharon Chanon Velazquez, who claimed her daughter had never hit Phoebe.

Angeles Chanon revealed her daughter had been suspended after an argument with Phoebe a month before her suicide. "She exchanged a couple of words with her," she said — but refused to say what her daughter had said in the confrontations with Phoebe. "My daughter never fought with her or said, 'Go harm yourself', or 'I hate you'."

Ms Chanon said her daughter had informed her about the dispute. "Phoebe was calling her names. They're teenagers. They call names," she told the *Boston Herald* newspaper.

One of Sean Mulveyhill's neighbours told a local newspaper she was shocked by the allegations. Shelley Lawrence said: "I know that he comes from a family that really cares about their children and is really involved with their children." Like much of South Hadley, she blamed the school's officials for not stepping in before Phoebe committed suicide.

Following the findings of the criminal investigation, Phoebe's death became a major talking point in the US. In mid-April of 2010, the hugely popular *People* magazine highlighted Phoebe's "bullicide" on the front page under the headline: 'Bullied To Death?' The magazine revealed the horrific details about what drove the 15-year-old to end her life. There were also reports that some of the accused received death threats.

Back in South Hadley, under-siege school officials did their best to stick to their guns, insisting that the school had done all it could to help Phoebe. Superintendent Gus Sayer claimed staff only became aware of the bullying one week before Phoebe's death. He said they took "very strong action" once they became aware of the abuse.

"We don't have knowledge of any bullying or other incidents before that," he said. "No-one turned their back on this. I think we did everything we could. If I thought I had done something wrong, I would resign. But I think we did our best."

But Northeastern DA Elizabeth Scheibel responded by saying that this was a lie, insisting the bullying suffered by Phoebe had been known to teaching staff.

Around this time, reports emerged that Phoebe's mother Anne had discussed her own fears that a gang of girls were a threat to her daughter with school officials in November 2009 — two months before her daughter took her own life. Anne contacted the school again in the first week of January 2010 to raise her fears that her daughter was being picked on.

Superintendent Sayer acknowledged that Ms O'Brien Prince had met a school nurse and a guidance counsellor — but claimed she did not bring up the bullying of her daughter.

Phoebe's father Jeremy said he believes his daughter may have downplayed her torment and felt there was no point in telling her family about the bullying. "Phoebe's perception — and I think it was the correct one — is that if she had told us, we would have been down at the school ranting and raving, but that the school would not do anything about it and it would actually get worse," he said.

It was also revealed that Phoebe's aunt Eileen Moore had sat down with a South Hadley High official before Phoebe enrolled and warned that she had been bullied before in Ireland and was "susceptible" to getting picked on by classmates. She made a point of urging the official to look out for her vulnerable niece.

When journalists put this fact to Superintendent Sayer, he

responded: "It is not appropriate for me to discuss anything from Phoebe's personal file."

But Eileen believes the school authorities could have done more to save her niece. "The signs were there and there was no support," she said. "If it can happen to an intelligent beautiful girl it can happen to anyone." She also said Phoebe "did not want to die" and "just snapped and had nowhere to turn".

"She wanted the pain to stop," Eileen said.

In May 2011, the trials of those accused of bullying Phoebe took place. Five of the accused agreed to plead guilty to lesser charges.

Sharon Velazquez, Flannery Mullins and Ashley Longe were sentenced to less than a year's probation. They had pleaded guilty to misdemeanor charges.

Similarly, Sean Mulveyhill and Kayla Narey were sentenced to 100 days of community service along with probation. The charge of statutory rape against Mulveyhill was dropped after he pleaded guilty to criminal harassment. The same charge was also dropped against Austin Renaud.

District Attorney David E Sullivan explained that the plea bargains were agreed "upon the request of the O'Brien-Prince family and in the interest of justice."

After the hearings, Phoebe's mother Anne said: "There is a dead weight that now sits permanently in my chest." She also described the last time she held her daughter in the crematorium a few days after the 15-year-old hanged herself.

"I lifted the lid of the coffin and held her for the very last time. My little girl, so very full of life, was now so cold."

Anne described her daughter as "beautiful, gregarious and kind-hearted", and listed some of her joys in life. These included the letters of Henry VIII to Anne Boleyn, reading with her parents and discussing literature with her mother. Those joys have all vanished, she added. "My kitchen table is a very quiet place to be these days."

Anne O'Brien also described trips to France in which Phoebe would run excitedly around markets, returning with her arms full of fruits and vegetables, a big smile on her face. A trip to France would only bring sadness now, the grieving mother said.

Displaying great courage, Phoebe's father Jeremy has also revealed that he is struggling to forgive the teenagers who made his daughter's life hell. In an interview with a US magazine, he said the teens have "already in some ways been punished," and that he saw little benefit in making an example out of them.

"There are levels of culpability among the kids," Jeremy said. "You want to see the law acknowledged, and reasonable penalties, but without making an example of them. You want to take their ages into account.

"There will always be younger ones who go with the flow and join in. There is no healing in anger, and there's no healing in revenge. The only real healing long-term can come from finding the ability to forgive. That right there has been my focus from the start. And believe me, it's bloody hard."

As time passes, Jeremy said it is simple things, like seeing grapes, Phoebe's favorite fruit, at the supermarket that continue to bring back the pain.

"It keeps coming back and it keeps hitting you and it keeps giving you immense distress."

One positive part of Phoebe's legacy, however, is the new anti-bullying law known as Phoebe's Law which was brought into being months after the Irish schoolgirl's suicide. The tough new law prohibits physical, emotional, and online taunting and mandates training for faculty and students. It also requires school staff to notify parents about incidents and harassment under the umbrella of bullying behavior.

Phoebe's aunt believes it would be a fitting tribute to the loving teenager who so needlessly lost her own chance at life. "I think her legacy will be to help other teens," Eileen said. "Her message would be that, 'You have to help the person who's being bullied get stronger'."

MICHAELA HARTE:
Murder in Mauritius

JOHN McAreavey clenched his fists in anguish as he wearily supported his head.

Just hours earlier that day, on January 10, 2011, the 26-year-old and his beautiful young bride had been sitting down to lunch by the pool in the luxurious Legends resort on the paradise island of Mauritius.

Now sitting in an interview room in a local police station on the island, not even the mounting pity in the eyes of the men interviewing him could help shake the feeling he was at least temporarily a suspect in his wife Michaela's murder.

A sense of utter desolation and loneliness enveloped the Co Down man.

Nothing mattered now... not the evaporating suspicions of his police interviewers nor the fact that he was utterly alone thousands of miles from home.

The memory of pulling his beautiful young bride — clad in only her swimsuit — from their hotel room bathtub was seared into his mind.

Stay with me Michaela, he'd urged her... he'd pleaded with her. But she was already gone.

He fleetingly allowed himself the thought that somehow all

this — his wife's death — was some kind of sick nightmare.

As he closed his eyes, the luxury of that thought — that he would somehow wake up and Michaela would again be at his side — comforted him for just an instant.

But the tortured young man had to open his eyes again.

His police interviewer coughed politely before requesting that devastated John run through the events of the day again.

That morning — the 11th since the couple were married — began with the two honeymooners waking to blazing sunshine pouring through the rear window of suite 1025.

The tropical mid-30°C sunshine had warmed the island's waters to almost bathing temperature, making the resort pool an inviting prospect for Michaela.

John, a non-golfer, had — with the sense of adventure shared by many a newlywed — signed up for a golf lesson.

After dressing, the couple had breakfast together and then went their separate ways — she to the pool and he to golf — after arranging to meet back at the poolside.

Michaela, somewhat uncharacteristically for the normally active young woman, lounged by the poolside awaiting John's return.

When he returned from his golf lesson the couple sat down to lunch at the Banyan poolside restaurant — a short 90-second walk from their room.

"After that, my wife ordered a tea," John said in his statement at the Criminal Investigation Division in Piton.

"And as she has the habit to have biscuits at the same time, she left me at the kiosk and went to our room to fetch some biscuits which were kept in the refrigerator," John told police.

"It was about 14.35 hours.

"I waited for her at the kiosk for about 15 minutes and the waiter had already served the tea and a cup of hot water but she did not [turn] up.

"I then went to my room to look for my wife ... I tried to open the door and noticed [it] was locked.

"As I left my key inside the room before going to have lunch, I could not open the door.

"I continuously knocked on the door but there was no response from my wife."

John said he then went to the reception to get a bellboy to open the door.

"As soon as the door was opened the bellboy left and then I entered the room," he recalled.

"I was shocked to see my wife lying in the bath which was filled with water and she was unconscious.

"I quickly removed her from the bathtub and placed her on the floor.

"I saw that she was senseless. I came out to seek help."

John said bellboy Rajiv Bhajun, who opened the door, was first to come to his assistance.

"I told him about the state of my wife and he entered the room to see her," he recalled.

"Then he phoned and asked for assistance."

Hotel manager Brice Lunot had been walking nearby when Rajiv grabbed him by the arm, half dragging him to room 1025, as he explained in a wild panic that the occupants desperately needed help.

Entering the room and witnessing the pitiful scene in front of him, Brice immediately began administering cardiac massage and CPR.

Later the hotel manager would recall that he noticed no sign of external injury on Michaela's body that would have caused him to think she had been the victim of a murder.

In those moments, as John sobbed pitifully beside him, Brice vowed to himself he would not leave the young Irishman's side until someone from Ireland could make their way to Mauritius to comfort and protect him in his loss.

That night — sitting in the corridor of the police station in Piton — Brice told the *Irish Daily Star* that he would not leave the young man to make his own way back to the hotel.

"John is very shocked and exhausted," he said. "I'm just waiting to take him back to the hotel.

"I didn't want to leave him alone in a foreign country after this has happened.

"It's a complete nightmare for him.

"I have no idea what happened [to Michaela].

"She was in her swimsuit ... my memory is not clear but I remember her eyes were closed and her body was very white.

"I'm not a doctor ... not a medical expert ... but I saw no trace of blood."

But John — who after five years together with his wife knew her probably better than anyone — had already come to the conclusion that she hadn't simply collapsed.

"It was obvious," he would recall later, "but I suppose I didn't really want to believe this.

"But it was evident, I knew somebody had done something."

Those suspicions had already been confirmed to police by chief medical officer Dr SK Gungadin who carried out an autopsy at the Victoria Hospital in Quatre Bornes on the night she was killed.

During his examination, he found the tragic 27-year-old's attacker had strangled her with such force that he had torn her skin in several places and also fractured a bone in her throat.

The horror findings in the four-page document, later obtained by the *Irish Daily Star*, show Michaela also suffered bruising and cuts to her head in her final moments.

During his examination, Dr Gungadin found several circular abrasions ranging from 0.5cm to 1.5cm in length, in a horizontal line in front of her neck.

He discovered several small patches of bruises of irregular shape and size in front of her neck, a 6cm x 4cm bruise over her right collarbone and a 5cm x 4cm bruise over her left collar bone.

He also found a number of cuts on her head as well as bruises to the left and right temporal areas of her head.

During the fatal attack, Dr Gungadin observed, her killer had fractured her hyoid bone — located in the centre of a person's neck near the larynx.

There could no longer be any doubt. Michaela had been

brutally murdered.

Dr Gungadin certified the cause of death as being "asphyxia due to compression of the neck".

More than 10,000km from the honeymoon suite where John McAreavey discovered his wife lying dead stands St Malachy's Church in Ballymacilroy, Co Tyrone.

The picturesque cream-painted building — surrounded by green fields and blue skies — held a special place in the hearts of Michaela and John.

There on December 30, 2010, the couple pledged to love, honour and obey each other until death did them part.

On that blissfully sunny day — just one day shy of Michaela's 27th birthday — no-one could, for one moment, have anticipated just how short a period those vows would be allowed to stand for.

Instead the entire parish had come out to celebrate with legendary Tyrone manager Mickey Harte on the marriage of his beloved daughter to her sweetheart of five years, John.

Not that Michaela hadn't already begun to shape a distinct character in the mind of the public.

Her appearance in the Rose of Tralee in 2004 had struck a chord with viewers up and down the country.

The poem she recited that night, Mairtin O Direain's Faoiseamh a Gheobhadsa (Peace of Mind) — with its lines as Gaeilge about "finding peace for a short time on a seaside island" — would years later prove eerily prophetic.

People said afterwards that although she hadn't won the contest outright that night, her appearance in the competition had won her a genuine affection in the hearts of the estimated 900,000 people who viewed it that year.

And even to those who didn't witness her on stage in the Dome in Tralee, Co Kerry, she had become a familiar sight at her father's side as the Tyrone senior footballers battled to bring the Sam Maguire Cup north of the border again following their triumph the year before.

"She loved being around the training and 'the boys' as she called them," Mickey fondly recalled of his daughter later.

"That's all she ever talked about in terms of the football because she felt they were more like brothers of hers. She and I had wonderful days together on the football scene."

On the day Mickey's Tyrone won their first All-Ireland — a September 2003 clash with footballing giants Armagh in front of 79,000 people in Croker — Mickey and his daughter shared perhaps their most special moment together on a football pitch.

"She and I kept the little pact that we had that I would speak to no-one until I spoke to her," Mickey would later recall.

And, of course, Mickey didn't.

Only somebody very special could ever hope to occupy a place in Michaela's heart — given the huge respect she held for her father. Her love of Gaelic football perhaps made it inevitable that the man she would ultimately fall in love with would be a footballer.

But nobody would have guessed this footballer would play for Down rather than her native Tyrone.

John McAreavey was studying for his second-year accountancy exams in Queen's University, Belfast, when a friend introduced them in the the Botanic Inn in Belfast in 2005.

The then 21-year-old was instantly smitten with teetotaller Michaela who was living her college years at St Mary's College, where she was studying to be a teacher.

Michaela's best friend Adele McCarron would recall that the house the pair shared with two other girls on Belfast's Rugby Avenue became known as the "Tea House" because the four would have parties after nights out.

Michaela would always ensure there was a good selection of tea, cakes and buns.

Although neither John nor Michaela lacked confidence, the Down minor was struck by the fact that Michaela's confidence gave her the poise to abstain from alcohol completely.

"It was quite nice," he would say later, "to meet somebody that was sure of themselves and when they're talking to you late at night it's going to be the same person that's talking to you in the morning time. I liked that in a person, she was the same person all the time."

Within three weeks of their meeting in The Botanic Inn, John and Michaela knew they had found their life partners.

After meeting John, Michaela became a fixture on the social scene in his home village of Lawrencetown, near Banbridge, Co Down.

She got a job teaching Irish in a school in Dungannon, while John found work as an accountant with Henry Murray & Co in Lurgan.

A family friend would later remark that as devoted to Tyrone and her father's cause as she was, Michaela gradually was giving up the red and white to come to live among the red and black.

While she remained living with her parents in Ballygawley until her wedding, Michaela enthusiastically got involved with the local GAA club in Lawrencetown, Tullylish, where John was captain of the senior football team.

Then on December 28, 2008, John flew Michaela to Paris to ask for her hand in marriage.

"I tried to surprise her, which I always wanted to do," he would recall in the months following his wife's death.

"I took her over to Paris and we were engaged on December 28, 2008.

"She probably knew by the time we got to Paris what was on the cards, although she said she didn't.

"The night we got over there we got engaged and had a lovely holiday and just started planning the wedding.

"In hindsight, I wish I would've got married much sooner but at the same time I was fortunate that Michaela would've spent a lot of her time down at my home anyway.

"In the five years that we were going out with each other, the most time we spent away from each other was three nights.

"So in many ways we got to experience that kind of lifestyle with each other.

"To get married these days and live in a house, it costs a lot of money and we had to do a lot of saving — save for a deposit for a house and then save money to get married."

Eventually the couple saved enough to buy their home together. They bought a detached property in a modest development on the outskirts of Banbridge, where houses were for sale from €140,000.

They had the house — which was just two miles from John's parents' home — landscaped and then invited John's team-mates from Tullylish to the house for tea as their housewarming.

For Mickey, his daughter's suitor was everything he could have hoped for in a young man and he welcomed John into the family as a son.

The morning of the wedding, the unbridled joy in the Hartes' house in Ballygawley was plain to see.

Best pal Adele recalled: "We were all in Michaela's room getting ready and they were practically hanging out the window singing 'Going to the chapel and we're going to get married' to Michaela's aunties and uncles and cousins."

Similarly, Mickey Harte's happiness was obvious in the church as he walked his daughter up the aisle that December morning.

With a final proud smile, he left her at John's side before the altar where John's uncle, the Bishop of Dromore, also John McAreavey, got the ceremony underway.

"It was a fantastic wedding," a family friend would say later.

"There was a lot of young people at it. It was a very happy wedding and the young people really enjoyed themselves, and so did John and Michaela."

The couple celebrated after the ceremony at the luxury Slieve Russell Hotel in Co Cavan.

It wasn't until two days later — on New Year's Day — that Mickey drove the couple to Dublin Airport to catch their honeymoon flight to Dubai from where they travelled on to Mauritius.

It was the last time he would ever see his daughter alive.

On January 10, and just hours after Michaela's death in Mauritius, police inspector Ranjit Jokhoo and his team of investigators at MCIT were coming under intense pressure to solve her murder.

MCIT — specifically set up to investigate serious crimes on the island — was assigned to take over the investigation from the regular detective unit based at the Criminal Investigation Division's headquarters in Piton.

Mr Jokhoo was supremely confident his team would catch Michaela's killers. His unit, he said, had an astonishingly high rate of success.

The previous year, according to Mr Jokhoo, there had been 39 murders in Mauritius, a country with a population of just over 1.2 million and every single one of them had been solved.

Mr Jokhoo and his detectives had not been the first police officers to arrive at the scene in the Legends resort that day.

The Criminal Investigation Division (CID) were and they initially suspected heartbroken groom John.

By the time Mr Jokhoo and his Major Crime Investigation Team arrived at the scene of the killing, the Down Gaelic footballer had already been taken to the CID's headquarters in Piton to be interviewed.

After a preliminary examination of the scene — and having ordered that everyone in the vicinity in the relevant window of time be interviewed — Inspector Jokhoo went straight to the local police station to speak with John.

"At that stage he was being interviewed by our local colleagues to ascertain if he was a suspect," Inspector Jokhoo recalled afterwards.

"We went to the station to observe him and talk to him to establish whether he was a suspect.

"I've been a police officer for 39 years and, like police all over the world, you have a deep understanding of human nature and an instinct.

"I knew within minutes, when I saw the distraught state he was in and the look in his eyes, the man sitting before me was totally innocent.

"You observe a person and their behaviour without letting them know you're doing so."

But Inspector Jokhoo's reaction was not, he said, based on gut instinct alone.

A number of witnesses had verified John's presence in the Banyan Restaurant up until the moment he left to go check on his wife.

And the porter who opened the door to room 1025 for John said the newlywed had started screaming for help a matter of seconds after entering the room.

These accounts led the MCIT to conclude it was a physical impossibility that John played any hand, act or part in his wife's death.

Furthermore, an examination of the hotel's key-card system showed a master card — which had been stolen from the resort security room on January 7 — had been used by someone to enter Michaela's room two minutes before she did.

Somebody else — most likely a staff member or members — had entered the hotel room just moments before Michaela did, and now Inspector Jokhoo and his team had to find out who and why.

Mr Jokhoo and his team knew they had to move with haste because, not least from a tourism point of view, the murder of Michaela Harte could spell a major economic headache for the Mauritian government.

Tourism accounts for nearly one tenth (8.7 per cent) of the country's gross domestic product — far outstripping the flow of income to the government's coffers from the formerly dominant sugar cane industry — which now lags some way behind, accounting for just over half that figure.

Mauritius had begun marketing itself as the ultimate paradise island honeymoon destination after the country gained independence from the British in 1968.

The island's business leaders had worked hard in promoting it as a venue for tourists from South Africa and a large number of western European countries including Ireland.

Headlines announcing that a killer was on the loose would dramatically affect the country's ability to market itself as a safe destination for young honeymooners.

Already — as word of Michaela's murder reached Ireland — signs advertising Mauritius as a honeymoon destination were being taken down from the windows of travel agents throughout the country.

The Mauritian government wanted those responsible for Michaela's death found as quickly as possible.

No resource was to be spared.

Police investigators from MCIT poured into the Legends resort — interviewing the resort's 600 staff.

Crime scene officers had sealed off the room and plastic bags had been placed on Michaela's head and feet in order to preserve DNA traces on the body.

Michaela's fingernails were clipped to see if DNA traces from her killers would be found beneath them and the room was then heavily dusted for fingerprints to see if her killers had left prints behind.

The scenes of crime officers also swabbed the tap handles of the bath and the wardrobes in the room.

As John was being escorted back to the hotel by caring hotel manager Brice Lunot, the investigation team used the hotel staff rosters to whittle down the list of suspects to those who were present on the day.

Mr Jokhoo would later reveal that by 11pm on the night Michaela had been killed, the police had statements from the barmen, other hotel workers and John McAreavey that allowed them to work out where every single staff member was at the time of the attack.

Just eight hours after the murder, the police had whittled down their list of likely killers to just three people.

Meanwhile, the results of the post-mortem carried out on Michaela at the island morgue in the town of Quatre Bornes were delivered to the MCIT.

Dr Gungadin's report confirmed Michaela had been murdered.

Now the police felt they had the ammunition they needed to go ahead and interview their suspects.

The first suspect that police would later allege had cracked and confessed to playing a role in the tragic killing was hotel cleaner Raj Theekoy (33).

"He knew he was a suspect in a murder and he told us he heard [Michaela] screaming inside room 1025 but he didn't do anything," Mr Jokhoo said later.

According to Mr Jokhoo, Theekoy volunteered that he had seen a cleaning trolley used by fellow cleaner Avinash Treebhoowoon parked outside the entrance to Michaela and John's room at the time of the murder — adding he had noted the door was closed at the time.

This breached the Legends Hotel's strict policy on cleaners leaving the door open behind them while they cleaned the room.

Confident they now had enough on Theekoy to charge him, at least provisionally, the police next moved on to Avinash Treebhoowoon — a cleaner who on the day of the murder was assigned to room 1025 and 11 other rooms.

Treebhoowoon (29) was, according to Inspector Jokhoo, quite open about his involvement in the killing when confronted with Theekoy's statement against him.

"They did not intend to kill her — we are certain of that now," Mr Jokhoo continued.

"Avinash said he had spotted a purse stuffed with money in the couple's honeymoon suite the day of their arrival and he was tempted by that."

The following day, the day of the murder, that purse "contained just €451 — €300 in notes, 3,500 Mauritian Rupees (€92) and stg£50," the inspector said.

But it was enough, he continued, to tempt the cleaner and the third suspect in the case, room supervisor Sandip Moneea (41) — who was also on duty in that section of the hotel — back into the room.

"He [Treebhoowoon] said he was rifling through the purse when Michaela entered the room," Mr Jokhoo continued.

"Michaela was foolish — she shouted at him 'What are you doing? What are you looking for?'.

"He says he panicked and pushed her back and she hit her head on the ground as she fell.

"Michaela was screaming as she got back to her feet and that's when the second man Sandip Moneea — he has not yet confessed — tried to gag her by putting his hand over her mouth.

"He also put his arm around her neck to drag her back and this is how her throat was compressed.

"It was at this stage that Michaela Harte fainted.

"They then picked her up and placed her in the bath with the water running and left the room."

Moneea was now the only suspect, according to police, to refuse to confess his guilt during interview.

But with the statement from the other two in the bag, the investigators felt they had enough to at least provisionally charge the three men.

The decision, based on the strength of the confessions alone as no DNA evidence and no CCTV footage capable of implicating the men had been found, was announced the night after the murder.

Within 36 hours of the killing, police were claiming to be satisified Michaela's killers were behind bars. The following morning the trio would appear before the magistrate at the crumbling courthouse in Mapou — 25km north of the capital Port Louis — to be charged in connection with the murder of Michaela Harte.

On Wednesday, January 12 — just hours after journalists and photographers from Ireland arrived in the country to witness it — the three men were marched into the courtroom in Mapou.

But an event intended to herald the police force's triumph over Michaela's killers was quickly to be overshadowed by bombshell claims that the confessions extracted from the suspects had been obtained through torture.

In the sweltering midday heat, all three accused looked shocked and stunned as they were escorted by police past their families and into the courtroom.

In the case of Avinash Treebhoowoon, tears streamed down his face as he was approached by relatives.

After the men were led into the court, the charges were read out in Creole — a French-based dialect that includes some words of English but also others from the many African languages.

Treebhoowoon and floor manager Moneea were provisionally charged with Michaela's murder, while Theekoy was charged with conspiracy to commit murder.

Moneea did not respond when charged with murder.

Raj Theekoy also did not comment when charged.

But Avinash Treebhoowoon — the youngest of the three men — immediately began gesturing to his face and speaking in Creole, indicating he had been beaten.

Treebhoowoon's lawyer Ravi Rutnah rose and demanded that his client be given an opportunity to speak.

Then, on being led to the stand, Treebhoowoon began talking very quickly — gesturing to his feet and hands in an excited fashion as he did so.

Gasps of horror could be heard in the courtroom as he proceeded.

His lawyer, Ravi Rutnah, helpfully offered to translate what his client had said. Mr Rutnah said his client was "stripped naked, held down on a table by officers and then beaten about the body and feet with pipes in order to coerce a confession from him".

He denied his client had made any confession to police.

Magistrate Sheila Bonomally paid careful attention to Treebhooowoon's evidence before remanding him and his co-accused in custody for another week.

She further ordered that Treebhoowoon be medically examined. That night the MCIT resolutely denied all allegations that Treebhoowoon had been tortured.

Over the following two days signed confessions were secured from both Theekoy and Threebhoowoon.

And with the three men now safely detained in custody, the police were frcc to focus in on their backgrounds.

The officers believed that the botched theft in Michaela's room was part of a petty thievery racket which Threebhowoon and Moneea had been involved in at the resort for some time.

They suspected the pair would have only taken a small amount of money from the cash from the wallet — €20 for example — hoping that Michaela and John would simply believe they had dropped the money somewhere during their travels.

They began to probe for signs of financial difficulty in the backgrounds of either man.

Soon enough they felt they had found thc motive they believed would help them link Moneea to the crime.

If Moneea had been stealing from hotel guests, a leaked government file prepared on him and the other suspects claimed he hadn't exactly been discreet about what he was doing with the money.

The room supervisor — who earned in the region of 10,000 rupees (€250) a month — had built himself a house on School Road in Petit Raffray that police estimated would have cost in the region of €25,000 to build.

According to the dossier on Moneea, he had met his wife Rekha four years earlier but they put off their wedding until he was able to build a house in which they could live together.

"He borrowed money, tens of thousands, and bought land in Petit Raffray," an investigation insider was quoted as saying.

"He then borrowed more money to build his big house on School Road.

"It is very big by Mauritian standards. The total cost of the land and house was one million rupees [€25,000].

"Sandip only earned 10,000 rupees (€250) per month working as a floor supervisor at the Legends Hotel and was finding it impossible to pay the loan sharks. So he started stealing from the hotel," the insider claimed.

"He had to find other ways to get money and the easiest way to do that was to rob hotel rooms.

"The week before the murder, he stole mobile phones from a number of other rooms, which he gave to the loan sharks."

Police said their main line of inquiry now was that Moneea was heading up the petty theft racket in order to pay back violent loan sharks from whom he had borrowed money.

They alleged that he was the one in a position of authority — adding he would easily have been able to coerce the likes of Treebhoowoon into going along with him.

The claims were put to Moneea but he steadfastly denied them. He hadn't been in the room, he repeatedly told police, he hadn't killed Michaela.

Moneea's wife echoed her husband's claims that he was absolutely innocent of any involvement in the crime and described the claims in the dossier as complete rubbish.

Rekha, who was due to celebrate her 40th day of marriage to Moneea the day after he was arrested, said: "He has been trapped to that case. I married Sandip on December 5 — today is our 40-day anniversary — and I would cut my throat before I would believe he has done this thing. God knows somebody has done this terrible thing but somebody else has done a foul thing in blaming my husband for this.

"How could my Sandip have done this?

"He was with me on Monday night and he came home like normal — same as every day.

"He was not worried — he was not upset.

"He helped me as he always does — we cooked food together and watered the plants and then we sat down together to say our prayers. These are not the actions of a killer."

Rekha continued that in 10 years of work at the hotel, her husband has never had a single complaint made against him.

She also pointed out that she too was earning "good money" by Mauritian standards — she worked in the Mauritian government's finance department — and so asked why her husband would ever steal.

"We were both on a good wage," she said. "There simply wasn't any need."

The wives of Avinash Treebhoowoon and Raj Theekoy would relate similar tales.

Reshma Treebhoowoon said she believed her husband Avinash's claims that he was savagely beaten in an effort to force a confession from him.

Raj Theekoy's wife Manisha also declared her husband's innocence.

"Raj," she said, "has never even been in a fight."

The families would be left stunned just days later when police confirmed that both Raj and Sandip had now put their confessions in writing.

Morning comes early for tourists visiting Mauritius.

A mixture of intense heat, blazing sunshine and the vast array of possibilities activity-wise normally force even the most reluctant visitor from their bed.

John McAreavey woke early on the Wednesday morning — two days after his wife was killed — for very different reasons.

That day his brother Brian and Michaela's brother Mark were to fly into Mauritius to help him organise the return of his sister's body to Ireland.

The day before, John had managed to have Michaela's rosary beads, as well as her engagement and wedding rings, returned to him.

And now — with no small amount of help from the Irish Department of Foreign Affairs — the grieving relatives had been told they could finally bring Michaela back home.

At roughly 11am, John McAreavey set out on the 17-mile journey from the Legends Hotel to the mortuary in the Princess Margaret Hospital to say goodbye and bring her remains home.

Taking possession of his sister's body that day, Mark Harte would detail the horror of the moment he learned his sister was dead right through to the nightmare journey to Mauritius to collect her remains.

In a signed statement to police, Mark (31) said: "Michaela Harte was my smaller sister and she came to Mauritius on holidays to the Legends Hotel in Grand Gaube ... together with her husband John James McAreavey."

"On Monday, January 10, during the evening I was in Ireland when I was informed by my relations that my sister had passed away and that a police inquiry was on and later I learnt that an autopsy was carried out.

"I came to Mauritius today Wednesday, January 12, to take over the body for repatriation with the support of the Irish embassy."

Mark's statement went on to say: "On January 10 at the Princess Margaret Orthopaedic Centre Mortuary House at 23.30 hours, the senior police medical officer carried out an autopsy ... and certified the cause of probable death as asphyxia due to compression of the neck.

"Now, after identification, you [police officers] are handing me over the body of my dead sister and I am taking it over.

"I take responsibility for the repatriation with the support of the Irish embassy to Ireland.

"It will be by flight MK042 on January 13, scheduled at about 22.30 hours.

"You are giving me a copy of the chief police medical officer's report. I do not know how my sister passed away.

"I have been informed that the inquiry is going on and its circumstances will be communicated to the relatives in due course."

Mark signed the statement at 6.55pm on Wednesday, January 12, 26 hours before he would fly home with his sister's body to their devastated family in Ireland.

Covered in a pink sleeve, Michaela's coffin was then removed from the morgue and brought to Sir Seewoosagur Ramgoolam Airport where paperwork was completed in order to send her body home.

Outside the morgue, John kept his head bowed — her two rings on a delicate gold chain visible around his neck.

Looking ashen-faced, his family then guided him into a car that had pulled up outside to bring him back to the Legends Hotel to wait for his flight home with his murdered bride that night.

John had yet to speak publicly in the wake of his wife's murder but the devastation he was feeling at her loss was laid bare for the first time in a statement released through his family.

In it, he said: "My beautiful wife, my best friend, my rock, Michaela, has been taken from me and I still can't take it in.

"Our hopes, our dreams and our future together are gone. I am heartbroken and like Mickey, Marian, Michaela's brothers and my family, I am totally devastated. I am numbed.

"I love my wife very, very much and my world revolved around her. I can't describe in words how lost I feel as Michaela is not just the light of my life — she is my life."

John also thanked the public for the support he had received.

"I appreciate all the prayers and messages of support," he said. "I pray that God gives us the strength and faith that Michaela has to cope with our horrific loss.

"She is a gift from God and I now have an angel."

The flight carrying Michaela's remains departed Mauritius at 10.20pm local time that night.

A day and a half later and after an exhausting series of flights that finally ended at 12.40pm on Friday afternoon, John accompanied Michaela's remains back to George Best Airport in

Belfast on a privately chartered flight from London Heathrow.

Her simple wooden coffin was immediately driven to the old terminal — far away from the bustle of the main airport building.

About 50 minutes later, a hearse from Quinn Undertakers — run by a family friend — arrived to take Michaela on the final stage of her sad journey home.

Her coffin was draped in a plain purple cloth — a simple and elegant reflection of the girl whose life had been so cruelly cut short.

Inconsolable, John barely glanced upwards as he waited anxiously for the hearse to begin their journey.

Sitting sombrely in the back seat of one of the six cars the families had arranged to escort Michaela back to Tyrone, the young widower appeared ashen-faced and drawn — a man whose heart has been totally torn apart.

Two PSNI motorcyclists provided the escort for the cavalcade of cars as it swept out of the airport.

Mickey Harte sat dejectedly hunched in the rear of the first car, his tear-stained face painfully illustrating the hurt and agony he had endured that week.

After pausing at a funeral parlour for a private removal service, the cavalcade finally reached Tyrone shortly after 7pm.

The darkening clouds and pouring rain earlier in the day had provided an apt setting.

The focal point of the grief was the Ballygawley roundabout.

Many of the hundreds of onlookers gathered there were clad in the distinctive white and red colours of the Tyrone team.

There was near silence as the cortege passed through, with members of Errigal Ciaran GAA providing a guard of honour.

Michaela was home ... back amongst her own.

In Mauritius the investigation into the act of evil that had destroyed John and Michaela's lives together would continue in John's absence.

By Thursday morning, police were now publicly stating that both Raj Theekoy and Avinash Treebhoowoon had confessed to their roles in the murder.

And in a move that seemed designed to court the media but in reality is something done regularly by police investigating murders in Mauritius, Police Commissioner Tishur Rampersad announced that both men would be reconstructing their alleged crimes at the Legends resort that very afternoon.

True to Mr Rampersad's promise, Treebhoowoon and Theekoy were driven at speed through the front gates of the five-star Legends resort shortly before 6pm local time to perform their re-enactment of the grisly murder.

The police's "main suspect" Treebhoowoon was the first to be taken from the police van in handcuffs to spend more than 30 minutes in room 1025.

Next, Theekoy was brought in to describe where he was when he heard Michaela's screams but did not go to her aid.

Afterwards, police said the re-enactment was vital in exposing inconsistencies between the men's stories that might help consolidate the case against them.

They said the case was now 100 per cent secure against all three men — including Moneea who continued to maintain his innocence — adding all three would face sentences ranging between 18 and 60 years in jail.

"The circumstantial evidence is overwhelming," a police source said. "All three men will spend a long time in jail."

The reconstruction that day was the first chance many of the Irish passport-carrying journalists had to view the inside of the Legends Hotel.

A lockdown — keeping out any new Irish guests for fear they worked for a newspaper in Ireland — had been in operation by resort management since the murder.

The days afterwards would also provide the first opportunities for which images could be obtained of the room in which the killing had taken place.

Pictures published in the following days would show the forensic nature in which the police had examined the room.

Blue finger-printing powder was clearly visible on the inside of the door and also on the inside of the bath in which Michaela had been found.

The bed sheets were unmade and a phone-cord lay strewn across the bed.

Yet more evidence, police might later argue, that the cleaners had been doing anything but their jobs during their time inside room 1025 on the day of the murder.

But, in spite of all the "overwhelming" evidence police claimed to have against the three men, the man officers said they believed carried out the actual act of strangling Michaela continued throughout that week and since to deny all involvement in her murder.

Speaking that weekend though, Inspector Jokhoo seemed unbothered by Sandip Moneea's insistence on his innocence. "He denies everything," Mr Jokhoo admitted.

"He says he did not go to the room.

"He says he was working in that sector because he is a supervisor there but he says he never entered the room itself."

The police investigation would continue in the days, weeks and months to come.

On January 18, a hotel security guard, Dassen Narayanen (26) was arrested by MCIT officers as he attended hospital to have a cast on his right ankle changed.

Narayanen — who said he had entered room 1025 after hearing John McAreavey cry out for help — was accused by police officers of involvement in a conspiracy to kill Michaela.

In a statement, he admitted first seeing another hotel worker, Seenarain Mungroo, writing on a hotel key card.

But in a subsequent statement, Narayanen altered his statement to clear Mungroo — previously a person he claimed was a friend.

The new statement — which Narayanen claims to have signed

only after a police officer held a gun to his head — stated that he had handed a stolen key card to alleged killer Sandip Moneea.

In an interview with the Irish Daily Star, Narayanen — whose charge of conspiracy to murder was later reduced to conspiracy to commit burglary — said neither statement is true.

The charge of conspiracy to commit burglary remains before the courts in Mauritius.

Narayanen's lawyer Poonum Sookum secured bail of 200,000 Mauritian rupees for her client on March 28.

Seenarain Mungroo was released from custody after Narayanen amended his original statement.

MCIT said they believe Narayanen set up Mungroo in retaliation over a complaint the latter made about Narayanen at the Legends resort, where both men worked, the previous year.

Somewhat unusually PSNI officers from the North travelled to Mauritius in March to liaise with the investigation team and report back to Ireland on how the investigation was going.

The officers concerned subsequently confirmed to Mickey Harte that they felt "happy with the investigation".

Some 19 days after Michaela and John's wedding in the small cream-coloured church in Ballymacilroy, Co Tyrone, the 27-year-old teacher was brought back to St Malachy's — clad once again in the white dress she had worn on her wedding day.

This time however, there was to be no joy and no laughter — the memories of Michaela leaning out her bedroom window singing "going to the chapel" on the morning of her wedding banished for fear they would bring strong men to their knees.

The faces of the more than one thousand mourners who turned out that cold but sunny mid-January morning to witness her arrival to the church in Ballygawley were all grim.

None more so than that of her young husband who — with anguish etched across his tear-stained face — tilted his head and tenderly kissed the coffin as it was being carried to the church.

Consoled by a heartbroken Mickey Harte, the devastated pair watched as a hearse took their special girl along the final few yards to St Malachy's Church.

Inside, footballers — hardened by countless League and Championship battles — unashamedly let the tears flow silently down their cheeks.

Michaela had been at their side during so many of those battles.

The players weren't just weeping for the manager's daughter.

They were weeping for one of their own.

Addressing the thousands of mourners who spilled out across the Tyrone countryside, Bishop McAreavey spoke movingly of the deep love and affection Michaela held for her family.

"The first love in Michaela's life was the love of her parents, Mickey and Marian, and her brothers, Mark, Michael and Mattie," he said.

"As everybody knows, Michaela was close to her dad, and through him became part of a wide circle of friends in Tyrone and in the GAA family throughout Ireland.

"Michaela was a Tyrone woman through and through and nothing was ever going to change that."

Bishop McAreavey said Michaela's murder had been "an evil act" which had robbed her husband of "a beautiful wife".

He added: "It deprived the Harte family of their precious daughter and sister; it deprived the McAreavey family of the daughter-in-law they looked forward to having; it shattered hopes and dreams for the future."

The first three days of the preliminary hearing in late June into the murder of Michaela were heard at the same courtroom in Mapou where Theekoy, Treebhoowoon and Moneea had been brought in early January.

No evidence would be heard in the opening week of the hearing because of continued motions by the defence seeking full discovery of all documents implicating their clients.

Instead the defence sought to capitalise on an absence of any CCTV or DNA implicating their clients.

A copy of the report on the DNA analysis obtained by the Irish Daily Star revealed no evidence implicating either Treebhoowoon or Moneea.

In the report prepared by Susan Woodroffe of Cellmark Forensic Services in Oxfordshire, she stated that on February 1 a number of items were received at their offices for analysis.

These included nail clippings from Michaela's hands, swabs from the plastic bags used by the forensic officers to preserve evidence, swabs from the buttons of the safe in the hotel, swabs from cupboard and wardrobe handles in the room and also from a magnetic room card recovered by police.

Her report noted of the plastic bag taken from Michaela's head — labelled JV1. "The bag was intact. There was light blood-staining covering the majority of the inner surface of the bag," she said.

It continued: "The DNA profiles of Michaela Harte and John McAreavey were present."

MCIT said this was expected as John had removed his wife from the bathtub after finding her and performed first aid.

It stated of the plastic bag taken from Michaela's left foot and her right foot, "There is no specific indication that any of John McAreavey, Raj Theekoy, Sandip Moneea, Avinash Treebhoowoon and Dassen Narayanen have contributed to the mixed profile [obtained]."

The only DNA matching any of the suspects found in the room was that of Dassen Narayanen — a security guard who is alleged to have passed on a key-card to Sandip Moneea— for the purposes of burgling the room.

But Narayanen said his DNA was present only because he went to John's aid in the immediate aftermath of his wife's death.

He said he pulled a towel from the wardrobe and wet it before offering it to John to help aid what Narayanen thought was an unconscious woman.

On day two of the preliminary hearing, the defence also hit out at police for claiming at a bail hearing on April 14 that CCTV existed incriminating Avinash Treebhoowoon.

Treebhoowoon was subsequently refused bail.

When prosecutor Mehdi Choony was requested to hand this evidence over to the defence, he said he was not aware that any such CCTV existed.

At the time of this book going to press, eyewitnesses — whom police claim will prove the guilt of both Treebhoowoon and Moneea — had yet to be called.

The list of witnesses includes "star witness" Raj Theekoy.

Inspector Jokhoo said Theekoy's statement and that of other key witnesses will result in both men being convicted.

The defence of Treebhoowoon, meanwhile, has sought leave from the Supreme Court in Mauritius for a judicial review on the grounds their client does not believe he will get a fair trial.

Michaela's loved ones have repeatedly stated they want only that the right men be brought to justice for her murder.

Speaking about his daughter's alleged killers earlier this year, Mickey Harte said: "The right people have to face justice.

"But I do feel satisfied that the police are on the right road — especially after the PSNI returned from Mauritius happy with the investigation. I have to trust them.

"But you know, this is a tragedy for everyone, including those men. I feel very sorry for them and their families.

"They've taken a life, they've ruined their own lives, they have ruined their families' lives and this is a legacy that will live on for a very long time, affecting many generations.

"Michaela's death is a tragedy for everyone, for the people who loved her and the people who murdered her."

MICHAEL DWYER:
Hitman or soldier of misfortune?

A SOLDIER of fortune hell-bent on inciting revolution in a poor South American country? Or a young man from a sleepy Irish village who got in over his head? When Tipperary man Michael Dwyer was found lying in a Bolivian hotel room in a pool of blood, dressed only in his underwear, a mystery began that would not seem out of place in a script for a Hollywood thriller.

What is not disputed is that the 24-year-old son of a middle-class Irish family was shot dead by a crack police unit in room 457 in the Hotel Las Americas in the city of Santa Cruz on April 16, 2009. But the circumstances of the shooting have ensured the controversy around Michael Dwyer's death endure to this day.

Bolivian President Evo Morales would like the world to believe that Michael was part of a well-trained, right-wing, extremist group who arrived in Bolivia with the sole intention of killing him, and plunging the country into civil war.

The popular left-wing president has claimed that he uncovered the details of their plot and sent in elite police officers to take down their terror cell.

Michael's family, however, fiercely deny that their son had anything to do with an assassination plot, and have poured scorn on the Bolivian authorities' version of events.

They believe their eldest son was executed in cold blood and their calls for an international inquiry have received the backing from politicians at home and within the European Union.

But what exactly was a young Irishman, fresh out of college, doing in South America with a group of hardened veterans, some of whom served in the Balkan wars?

Two of Michael's colleagues, who were also killed on that fateful April day, included a Bolivian with Hungarian and Croatian passports; 49-year-old Eduardo Rozsa-Flores, who led a group of 380 foreigners in the fight for Croatian freedom in the 1990s, and Arpad Magyarosi (29), a Romanian with Hungarian citizenship.

Rozsa-Flores was a shady character with links to a far-right group suspected of attacking indigenous Bolivians. He had also been implicated in ethnic cleansing claims in former Yugoslavia.

After Michael's death, a video emerged of the war veteran, in which he claimed to be in Bolivia to organise self-defence groups to take on pro-government elements. So, just how did the Irishman from the rolling hills of Tipperary end up associating with such a dangerous group of people?

It was a Friday afternoon in mid-April at the Dwyer family home in north Co Tipperary when the phone rang.

It was a journalist asking Martin Dwyer, an electrician and father-of-four, whether he had a son residing in South America. Mr Dwyer said he did. A few moments later the phone rang again. It was another journalist who told the family that it appeared their beloved son had been killed in a gun battle 6,000 miles away.

In the hours that followed, the Dwyers, a respected family who are well-regarded in their locality, were plunged into a crisis that they have never fully escaped from.

Photographs showing their son's bloodied body after he had been shot began to emerge. Media converged on their bungalow, everyone wanting to know whether the allegations from the Bolivian authorities were true.

Was Michael a paid mercenary killed after a botched assassination attempt on the country's president?

"We didn't know what was happening," Martin Dwyer said. "We had no confirmation of anything. This whole thing was blowing up in public and we had no idea what was going on."

As the bodies of the three men were displayed on national television, Bolivian authorities claimed to have foiled a terrorist mercenary plot to kill Evo Morales.

Police officials went on television and said Michael and his associates had been involved in a plot to blow up the president on a boat on Lake Titicaca.

The Bolivian authorities said the men had planned to attach explosives to a boat before Morales and his cabinet were to travel on it two weeks earlier near the Peru-Bolivia border.

The authorities also said the men had planted explosives at the house of a cardinal and had planned to attack Ruben Costas, an opposition politician.

A raid of the men's hotel in the opposition stronghold of Santa Cruz was given the green light and after an alleged 30-minute shootout, three of the gang were dead, and another two had been arrested.

A storage facility in a nearby park was duly raided and police confiscated explosives, high-calibre scoped weapons and what appeared to be travel plans for President Morales's motorcade.

The haul included C-4 explosives, which according to the country's vice president, Alvaro Garcia, "did not exist in Bolivia". Documents were also seized "pertaining not only to past events but future attacks against the highest authorities of the national government," Garcia added and the police were still searching for other suspects. "There are other cells," the vice president insisted.

The following day, President Evo Morales told journalists in the seaside town of Cumana: "I had information several days ago that they were preparing an assassination attempt. Yesterday, I gave the vice president and the commander of the national police instructions to stage an operation and detain those mercenaries."

In the aftermath of the shootings, the Bolivian media went - into overdrive, painting the group as dangerous extremists.

Michael was described as "an expert in martial arts and weapons". *La Prensa*, a popular Bolivian newspaper, described the Irishman as a soldier of fortune who fought in the international brigade of the right-wing Croatian Liberation Movement during the Yugoslav conflicts. This was despite the fact that Michael was no more than a boy when this conflict raged during the 1990s.

Personal details on Michael's social networking sites were seized upon and a portrait emerged of a man obsessed with guns and assassins.

The Tipperary man described himself as a martial arts enthusiast with an interest in kickboxing and Krav Maga — a form of hand-to-hand combat used by the Israeli armed forces.

He had taken part in quizzes on Bebo asking what type of assassin he would be. In Michael's case the answer was the Jackal, the name of the main character in Frederick Forsyth's novel about a plot to kill former French President Charles de Gaulle.

He was also quizzed on the type of fighter he would be, the answer: submission artist, and what military niche he would occupy. The answer: a sniper.

He was pictured in a variety of camouflage gear and carrying a range of "air weapons" on his page's photograph section. There were also claims that he had a tattoo on his shoulder with a fascist Nazi symbol.

But far from being a gun-toting hitman for hire, his family said he was a gentle and loving sort whose personality was as far away from the constructed hardman image as possible.

Michael, they said, was dedicated to his family and was particularly close to his two sisters, Aisling (25) and Ciara (24), while he doted on younger brother Emmet (16).

"He was larger-than-life in every respect. Everything would

be 100 decibels. He'd either be chasing his younger brother around the house, or putting his arms around you if you were cooking," explained his mother, Caroline.

"He was a real father figure to his brother. He'd bring him over to Galway for weekends…he was just very generous with his time, and was always there for his family and friends," his mother added.

His heartbroken father said their pain was made all the worse by the "character assassination" of their son following his death.

"Losing your son is difficult, but all that stuff has been just as bad. It's been very upsetting for the whole family. His reputation has been destroyed. That image just isn't true," he said.

Most of the claims had a simple explanation, according to Martin. The military-style pictures, for example, were from an Airsoft game involving a form of air rifle that Michael took part in with friends.

Speaking after Michael's death, Conor Scolard, chairman of the Irish Airsoft Association, confirmed the Tipperary man had attended events in Galway. "I wouldn't call him a serious enthusiast because he has the cheapest of guns," he said.

Mr Scolard also said that the sport is in no way a stepping stone to involvement with live weapons. He said: "We try to stay from real steel as much as possible. We have got advice from army trainers that handling an air-soft gun is about as realistic as a hurley. They are not comparable to the real thing."

And Michael's alleged SS tattoo was in fact a Celtic tribal symbol that he chose with his Brazilian girlfriend, and his dad insisted his son had never shown any interest in politics, neither national nor international, when he was growing up.

His mother too spoke of her shock that Michael had been painted as a man involved in international espionage and she ruled out any link to extreme political ideology. "That he knowingly was part of a plot to kill the president of Bolivia astounds me," she said. "Our family, inclusive of Michael, has never taken but a passing interest in politics, even at a national level. Our kitchen-table talk centred more on football and hurling and family, rather than politics and world affairs."

While some of the more knee-jerk accusations were successfully explained away in the weeks and months following Michael's death, other issues and information that subsequently emerged proved to be more troublesome.

For example, photographs taken of Michael in Bolivia posing with handguns and a rifle shocked even his parents.

In one photo, released by the Bolivian authorities, Michael is seen posing with what seems to be two-semi automatic pistols tucked into his trousers and two in his hands.

Another photo showed Michael and Rozsa-Flores, widely accepted as leader of the group, sitting in front of a table of handguns and bullets with the writing "Happy New Year 2009" and an arrow pointing to a sniper bullet.

So who exactly was Eduardo Rozsa-Flores and how did Michael come to be involved with him in one of the poorest and most politically unstable countries in South America?

To answer this question we need to travel to one of the most remote outlying corners of Ireland — Rossport, Co Mayo.

Before leaving for South America, Michael had just graduated with an honours degree in construction management studies at Galway-Mayo Institute of Technology.

He had worked in a few pubs throughout college and, later, as a doorman. As part of his work experience, he was involved in a construction management job in Dublin.

While waiting for his college results, he landed a six-month job as team leader with Integrated Risk Management Services (IRMS) at the Shell gas pipeline site in Co Mayo. IRMS are a well-known company based in Naas, Co Kildare, and headed by a former member of the Army Ranger Wing, Jim Farrell.

The company provided security for the site which was the focus of controversial protests by locals who were angry at the location of the gas project.

Working with IRMS, Michael was based at the compound surrounding the intended landfall for the Corrib gas pipeline at Glengad beach in Erris and it is here that he met and formed a friendship with a Hungarian associate of Rozsa-Flores.

A former colleague who also worked at the site, but who wished to remain anonymous, described Michael as a "likeable sort of guy, a bit naive but certainly not a killer. He was just a young man fascinated by all things military. He loved to dress up. He was involved in the security of the Shell pipeline and there he would have come into contact with people from Hungary and Poland with a military background and could have had his head turned, but he wasn't a leader, he was a follower".

When his contract with IRMS finished in October 2008, Michael returned home, telling his parents he was going to Bolivia in November for two months to take part in a bodyguard course with some others he had met through his security work. The group travelled first to Madrid, Spain, and then on to Bolivia and this is where Michael is understood to have first come into contact with Rozsa-Flores, later adding him as a friend on Facebook.

Born in Santa Cruz in 1960 to a Hungarian father and Spanish mother, Rozsa-Flores's family moved to Chile in 1972, then to Sweden and, in 1975, to Hungary.

He fought in the Croatian war in the early 1990s and was also a spokesman for a dissident organisation calling itself Iraqi Independent Government. Rozsa-Flores was a maverick and had travelled to Bolivia with the publicly stated aim of organising self-defence groups against the government's rule.

He also clearly understood that his mission would be dangerous because he outlined his plans to a Hungarian journalist and asked that the footage be released in the event of his death.

Speaking after the Santa Cruz deaths, a close friend of Rozsa-Flores's, Zoltan Brady, confirmed that he had gone to Bolivia "to fight against its communist government".

Brady revealed that: "Eduardo lived in the jungle and was involved in regular fights. He was a soldier, a partisan, fighting together with thousands of others in the jungle."

Exactly how much Michael Dwyer knew about his

colleagues' activities will never be known. But in correspondence to friends and family sent after his arrival to Bolivia, he revealed that the bodyguard course he had hoped to attend never materialised, but said he was staying on because the economic climate at home was bad, and that he had the prospect of security work.

The security work seems to have involved Michael acting as a bodyguard to Rozsa-Flores. But far from being in the inner circle of the group, Michael — who spoke scant Spanish and no Hungarian — seems to have been oblivious to what was really going on and seemed more interested in earning money.

In an email to his mother sent in February 2009, he referred to his new job, writing: "Not bad at all the guy really just has me for show most. Rich people!!!!!! His favourite line when someone asks who I am is, im his personal bodyguard."

He later boasted on his Bebo page that he was "happiest when cruising in my new BMW in South America".

Michael's father believes his son would never have consorted with Rozsa-Flores had he known the reality of what was going on. "I think it was just a job to him. If he knew there was something illegal or chancy about it, he wouldn't have done it. I'm 100 per cent about that," he said.

After arriving in Bolivia, Michael met a Brazilian woman, Rafeala Cotrim Moreira (27). The medical student later revealed how the couple met weeks before Christmas in 2008 and began seeing each other. Both were quickly smitten.

"He was different to every other man I knew. He was very attentive and respectful, always happy. You never saw him sad or giving out. I presented him to many people and everyone liked him. There was nothing not to like," she said.

Michael told his new girlfriend he was employed as a bodyguard. But she wondered why a European would work in Bolivia, South America's poorest and most backward country. He told her that the economic situation in Ireland was bad and that many of his friends were losing their jobs, and at least in Santa Cruz he had work and the cost of living was low.

Tellingly, Rafeala also said that Michael was totally unaware of the tense political situation in Bolivia involving the relatively wealthy lowlanders of European descent around Santa Cruz and the indigenous population, of which President Morales was descended, in the Andean highlands to the west.

She said he spoke only rudimentary Spanish and was always asking her to translate conversations with her friends into English. And she refuted suggestions that he was a racist or held fascist political views.

"When we would meet my indigenous Bolivian friends he never showed any hint of prejudice," she said.

Rafeala also said that had she harboured any doubts about what Michael was up to in Bolivia she would have ended their relationship immediately. "I had one goal which was to qualify and I would do nothing to put this at risk. But I never felt any danger or risk with Mike," she explained.

But much like Michael's parents, she was deeply confused when she saw the photos of her boyfriend posing with an array of weapons that came to light after his death. "This is the big problem. But I do not know in what context these photos were taken. I do not think the photos alone prove what they are trying to claim about Mike and until today the only thing against him is the photos. But to say someone is a terrorist or planned to kill the president you need more proof," she said.

And what of the man that Michael told his girlfriend he was working for, Eduardo Rozsa-Flores? Rafeala said she only met him once and found him friendly as they hung out in a bowling alley. But she remembers that despite Michael's presence, he spoke with the other members of their group in Hungarian.

If questions continue to swirl around what Michael was doing in Bolivia, there are even more hovering over the circumstances of his death.

What we know as fact is that on April 16, 2009, at around 4am, elite officers in green helmets and flak jackets burst into the hotel where Michael and the others were staying on the fourth floor. Authorities claimed they were greeted with gunfire and that a 30-minute shootout occurred.

Speaking afterwards, the head of the Bolivian police Victor Escobar claimed Michael and two others opened fire and had "machine guns and explosives" in their possession.

Two other people survived the raid. Mario Francisco Tadik Astorga (58), a Bolivian-Croatian, who also fought in the Balkans, and Elot Toazo, a Hungarian computer expert. They have been in custody ever since, held in a maximum-security prison without trial.

In the aftermath of the shootings, Bolivian authorities launched a media blitz to try and convince the international community that its security forces had acted in defence of the country's president.

Morales himself claimed the discovery of a suspicious car at the hotel was one clue that had led to the shootings, explaining that the car had been spotted at the scene of a bomb attack days beforehand on the unoccupied house of a local Catholic cardinal.

"A bomb was put at the house, the licence plate of the car was noted and later that car was found at the hotel," he said.

He also pointed the finger at the US, claiming its embassy in La Paz had been involved in the plot and called on President Barack Obama to distance himself from the plot. The US president responded by saying he was unfamiliar with the incident.

The Bolivian authorities also announced that they wanted to interview three men living in Ireland, whom they said had links to Michael Dwyer.

The men, two Hungarians and a Slovak, had travelled to Bolivia but returned to Ireland after the bodyguard course all four had hoped to partake in did not materialise.

The Hungarian man is known to have been linked, along with Rozsa-Flores, to the Szekler Legion, which wants autonomy for Hungarians in Romania.

The Bolivians claimed this man had previous experience in putting together "irregular groups" and it was he who first befriended Michael and later organised the trip to Bolivia.

But opposition politicians instantly rounded on the president, accusing the authorities of a set-up.

Senate leader Oscar Ortiz said: "From what's coming out, there was no shootout, just an execution. This is serious and shows there's something hidden here."

Santa Cruz governor Ruben Costas, who had in the past clashed with Morales, said he doubted the government's version of events. "This has been cheaply staged; this is a show," he said.

As the days passed and Michael's body was flown home for an emotional funeral, more cracks began to appear in the official version of events. Confusion reigned as to exactly what occurred during the police operation. Police said they had first used explosives to blow open the doors of the two rooms, before shooting broke out. But witnesses told local press of hearing four shots before a series of detonations rocked the hotel.

In a further blow to the government's credibility on the matter, the manager of the hotel where the incident happened publicly questioned the authorities' explanation of events.

Hernan Rossel, general manager of the Las Americas Hotel, said there were no guns in the room where Michael was shot.

"The police told me he had guns but I saw nothing. They told me a lot of weapons had been found in the furniture. They said the men were terrorists and a special police force had come from La Paz, the Bolivian capital, to eliminate them because they had too many guns and bombs," he said.

He also gave a graphic description of the carnage left in the wake of the police raid, saying: "The scene was horrific. I could hardly bare to look at the victims. I saw the Irishman lying on the floor with his face up and only wearing his underpants. There were many bullet wounds in his chest and his face was clean and I could see he was a young man."

Questions were also raised as to why none of the 30-strong police force were injured in what was described as a 30-minute shootout and why all the bullet holes on the fourth floor were inside the bedrooms, with none appearing to be the result of gunfire fired from inside the room towards the police in the corridors.

Claims by the hotel manager that cops had blocked the building's security cameras around an hour before the assault were also backed up by local news agency El Deber who reported the CCTV cameras were disabled before police launched their early-morning assault.

Six months after Michael's death, Ireland's State Pathologist Marie Cassidy told a packed coroner's court that Dwyer had been killed by a single shot to the heart.

Most likely, it was a shot from above, indicating that he had been lying down in bed. She said the bullet used, known as a "dumdum" bullet, was designed to cause massive internal damage to the target, literally "stopping them dead in their tracks".

This contradicted the findings of Bolivian authorities who claimed Dwyer was shot six times. Bolivian authorities also said that Dwyer had two guns in his room and that gunshot residue was found on him. However, Dr Cassidy, who carried out her own examination, had found no evidence of this.

At last, the Dwyer family were beginning to see some of the many contradictions in the events surrounding their son's death made public.

"The man on the street can see he was executed," said Caroline Dwyer at the time. "You don't have to be a ballistics or forensics expert to see that."

Michael's father said he hoped the findings of the inquest would alter the perception of some people that his son was involved in dangerous illegal activity.

"These details will change people's minds, especially those who had doubts. We've waited six months to get official confirmation of these details, and now we have them," he said.

But while the inquest was a closure of sorts, the Dwyers still felt that the full truth would never be established unless there was an international investigation into the deaths.

"We're stuck and can't move until we get those answer," added Caroline. But any hopes that the Bolivian government would be shamed into ordering such an investigation were short-lived.

Just days later hopes for an independent inquiry into Michael's killing were dealt a blow when a local Bolivian investigator said his government was not "obliged" to co-operate. Despite the mounting evidence that parts of the official police version of events had been fabricated, the official, Cesar Navarro, insisted Michael and his associates had travelled to Bolivia to "cause terror and blow up bombs".

"These people didn't come here as tourists, they came here to cause terror," said Navarro, who is head of the government probe into the killings.

The Dwyers, however, were not giving up and appealed to the Irish government to support their calls for an independent inquiry.

Already, the then European Minister, Dick Roche, had downplayed Michael's involvement in any plot to kill the Bolivian president, saying: "24-year-olds do not trot around the world and the fact they are wearing military garb doesn't necessarily mean they have military involvement."

Roche also expressed surprise that a photograph of one of the bodies of the dead men had shown his hands were tied.

"His hands were clearly tied in front. That is most unusual. If you are moving a body from a scene, I cannot understand the basis on which the hands would be tied," he said.

The governments of Hungary, Romania, and Croatia also joined Ireland in calls for a "full and impartial" account of events. Then Foreign Affairs Minister Micheal Martin said in May 2009: "The Irish Government has a legitimate right to seek facts of how one of its citizens came to be killed by the security forces of another state."

In December 2009, president Evo Morales was re-elected with a landslide victory in a vote that also saw his left-wing party set to dominate congress. The lead-up to the vote had often threatened to spill over into open conflict as the country's east and west vied for control over the future direction of the impoverished country. During his six-month stay in Bolivia, those closest to Michael say he was unaware of these tensions, despite the fact that this was the reason Rozsa- Flores, a Santa Cruz native, was back in the region.

The opposition responded to the election loss by saying its campaign suffered after the government claimed leading opposition figures in Santa Cruz, a ramshackle boomtown on Bolivia's tropical eastern plains that is the engine of the economy, were linked to a supposed terrorist group plotting to kill Morales.

Such assassination claims made by Morales and his team are nothing new. A member of the Aymara indigenous group, Morales was Bolivia's first Indian president since the Spanish arrived in the country more than 470 years earlier.

Born in a mining village, he herded llamas as a young boy, where his family grew coca, which is used in the production of cocaine but is also an important traditional crop in the region. In the 1980s, he emerged as leader of the coca growers and gained prominence in the 1990s in the struggle against the US-supported coca-eradication programme.

He formed the Movement Toward Socialism in 1995 and won a seat in the Bolivian congress in 1997. An outspoken critic of the government in Bolivia's turbulent politics, he was expelled from congress in 2002. However, he went on to win the presidential race in 2005, becoming the first person of indigenous descent to be elected president.

A popular leader fiercely critical of the US, he delivered on promises to bring his nation more of the profits from their oil and gas reserves after nationalising the industry.

Before he took office in 2005, Bolivia, a nation of some 10 million people, received $300m from oil and gas exports. After he nationalised production, that figure rose to $2bn.

But his reforming anti-capitalist ways have not gone down well with some sections of the country, in particular the light-skinned elite of European descent.

There were violent outbreaks in the country in both 2007 and 2008, including a coup d'etat attempt which Morales claimed was backed by the US.

But paranoia has also seeped into the ruling party's psyche

and Morales has made several claims of assassination plots against him, none of which were ever proven.

One incident saw two teenagers with a disused gun arrested in Santa Cruz, amid government claims that "terrorists with a telescopic sight rifle" were trying to kill the Bolivian leader.

The pair were later quietly released after it emerged that the gun could not be fired and they were over 2km from the airport.

In April 2010, it was now more than a year since the death of their son. The Dwyers grew increasingly frustrated with both the Irish and Bolivian authorities over the failure to establish an investigation into circumstances surrounding Michael's death.

Despite assurances, a spokesperson for the family revealed that the Irish ambassador to Argentina had not yet travelled to Bolivia.

"They feel disappointed that the ambassador has not yet travelled down. The longer such an engagement is delayed, they feel the lower down the priority the issue will become for all authorities involved," the spokesperson said.

Refusing to allow their son's death to drift into the background, Michael's mother Caroline travelled to Brussels in Belgium in May of that year and pressed MEPs to back her calls for a full investigation.

In an emotional address to the European Parliament, Caroline told MEPs that her son went to Bolivia to undertake a course in personal security, took work as a bodyguard and joked that his employer had more money than sense.

She added that his Brazilian girlfriend, Rafeala, believed his main downfall was his lack of understanding of the Spanish language.

In a major boost to their campaign, MEPs agreed to lobby the First-Vice-President of the European Commission, Catherine Ashton, to support the Irish Government's demands for a full inquiry.

A statement indicating support for an independent investigation would be a powerful statement that the EU is prepared to support the loved ones of citizens who have died in such tragic circumstances, a draft letter signed by MEPs said.

In response to this letter, Catherine Ashton said her office had raised the scandal of the deaths with senior Bolivian government officials but she stopped short of joining calls for an independent investigation into the deaths.

Undeterred, the Dwyers, with the support of the Minister for Foreign Affairs, wrote to the United Nations' Special Rapporteur on extrajudicial executions, Christof Heyns, to support their calls for an inquiry, pointing out a lengthy list of inconsistencies in the Bolivian version of events.

In a 28-page submission, the Dwyer family stated eyewitness and video evidence, along with autopsy and ballistic reports, contradict the Bolivian government's assertion that their son was killed in an armed confrontation with police.

They said their evidence proves there was no shootout, just a cold-blooded execution. According to the Department of Foreign Affairs, the Special Rapporteur, whose mandate includes communications with governments about alleged unlawful killings, is expected to present his response to the dossier to the Human Rights Council in June 2011.

While the Dwyers wait to see what the findings of this report might be, they will have been no doubt been buoyed by the revelations from the United States that Michael may have been lured to his death as part of a plot by Bolivia's own intelligence service.

In January 2011, Wikileaks — a website that publishes sensitive documents — released a diplomatic cable from the US embassy in La Paz which quoted a local source as saying that the group Dwyer was with had been hired by Bolivian intelligence to mount a phoney terrorist campaign.

This would then be used to justify the persecution of Morales's opponents. The source told diplomats that Dwyer and the other two people were shot dead in order to "erase tracks".

The cable said the embassy could not verify the claims but described the source as well-placed and reliable.

Hitman or soldier of misfortune?

The cable was sent a month after Michael's death and was provided to Spanish daily newspaper *El Pais*, which waited some time before publishing extracts.

Bolivia's interior minister, Sacha Llorenti, dismissed the leaked cable as "gossip".

But only a few weeks later, more disturbing information emerged, when, in February 2011, a key witness in the shooting, Ignacio Villa Vargas, went on Bolivian national television and claimed he had been tortured into admitting his role in the plot.

Vargas showed marks on his body, which he claimed were inflicted on him to force a confession — implicating Michael in terrorism. Vargas had been arrested in the days after the shooting, but later went on the run. During his television interview he confirmed that Rozsa-Flores did indeed head a group whose aim it was to partition Bolivia.

"That is not a lie," he said. But he added that investigators had tortured him with electric cables into confessing that the country's political opposition was behind the plot.

A spokesman for the Bolivian government ignored the claims of torture and instead seized on his statement that a group with the intention of dividing the country did exist.

As the seemingly never-ending culture of claim and counter claim continues, Michael Dwyer's family and friends still grieve for their loss.

Coming to terms with his passing has been made all the harder by the fact that they will never know exactly how much Michael knew about the plot to cause strife in Bolivia, or if he even knew anything at all.

The Dwyers are still fighting for the right to know how their son died and to hold his killers to account.

His girlfriend, who fled Bolivia after Michael's death, has re-enrolled in medical school in Brazil, but she too is still wracked by a question: "What if?"

Speaking a year after his death, she said: "Normally if it was late he would spend the night with me but this time he didn't. Now I can't help thinking what would have happened if I had asked him to stay. Would he be alive? I don't know.

"There is nothing I can do to bring him back. But I think of his family and what they have had to go through. He spoke of them all the time. So for their sake I want to tell you what he was really like. He was not just anyone. I wanted to be with him. I saw in him someone I sought in my life."

TRAGIC HOMECOMING: Celine's family collect her body after it was flown home from Spain to Dublin Airport

BRUTAL DEATH: Celine was beaten to death in front of her kids. (Below) Killer Paul Hickey at courthouse and (inset) on floor of a police car

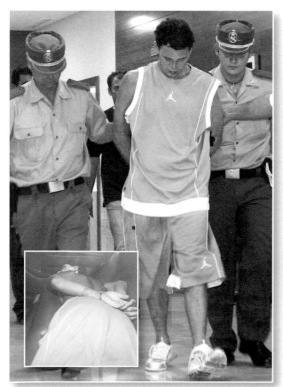

MOTHER'S GRIEF: Sandra Conroy weeps over the coffin of her daughter at a Mass in the Dublin Airport mortuary

117

TERRIFIED: Margaret weeps
in a video released by the Iraqi
kidnappers and (below) aired on
Al Jazeera television

ANGEL OF BAGHDAD: Slain Irish hostage
Margaret Hassan and (below) then Taoiseach
Bertie Ahern speaks at news conference with
her sisters Kathryn, Deirdre and Geraldine

PURE EVIL: French serial killer Pierre Chanal (above and top left) killed himself before he could be convicted for the murder of Irish teenager Trevor O'Keeffe in 1987

TAKEN TOO SOON: Trevor prepares to set out from his home in Naas, Co Kildare, and (above) his mum Eroline and sister Judith at court for Chanal's 2003 trial

119

MENTAL TORMENT:
Irish teen Phoebe
Prince, (left) her father
Jeremy and (below)
South Hadley High

VICIOUS BULLYING: The South Hadley High students
involved in the Phoebe Prince bullying investigation, (right,
from top) Sharon Chanon Velazquez, Flannery Mullins,
Ashley Longe, Kayla Narey, Sean Mulveyhill, Austin Renaud

120

SUSPECTS: Avinash Treebhoowoon, Raj Theekoy and Sandip Moneea in Mauritius

LIFE FULL OF LOVE: (Top) John McAreavey and Michaela Harte are married just days before her killing, and (above) GAA-mad Michaela joins Tyrone manager dad Mickey at 2003 All Ireland Senior Football Final

COUNTY IN MOURNING: Thousands paid their last respects at Michaela's funeral in Ballygawley, Co Tyrone

CONTROVERSY: Bolivian police claim Michael Dwyer was a hired gun in the country to help kill the president. He was gunned down in a hotel alongside (right) shady mercenary Eduardo Flores

PAINFUL MYSTERY: Michael's mum Caroline, brother Emmet, sister Aisling and father Martin Snr leave his death inquest. They deny he was part of any plot.

LOVING FAMILY: Lynsey (far right)
with mum Sandra, dad Paul, sisters
Keeley and Imelda and brother Dean

TEARS FOR THEIR FRIEND: Lynsey's friends from Loreto College Beaufort
pay their respects outside her home in Terenure, south Dublin

123

DAY OF INFAMY: Many Irish and Irish Americans were killed when terrorists hijacked airliners on the morning of September 11, 2001 and launched coordinated suicide attacks on the World Trade Center in New York and the Pentagon complex

SAD FATE: Ruth McCourt and her daughter Juliana died on 9/11, but her brother Ronnie (top) escaped towers

LIVES CUT SHORT: (Left to right) Carpenter Martin Coughlan, construction worker Kieran Gorman and stockbroker AnneMarie McHugh all died in the World Trade Center on 9/11. (Below) Rescuers carry FDNY chaplain Fr Mychal Judge

VANISHED WITHOUT A TRACE: Amy Fitzpatrick and (above) the track that the Irish teenager was taking on New Year's Day 2008

SORROW: Amy's pal Ashling Rose with her mum Debbie and (below) Amy's dad Christopher

HEARTBREAKING SEARCH: Amy's mother Audrey Fitzpatrick and her partner Dave Mahon

GANGLAND BETRAYAL: Westies bosses Shane Coates and Stephen Sugg and (below) their three henchmen: Stephen's brother Bernard 'Verb' Sugg and the Glennon brothers, Mark and Andrew — who eventually turned on the Westies

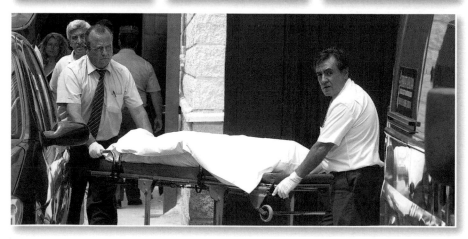

END OF THE LINE: Spanish police recover the buried bodies of Sugg and Coates

127

YOUNG AND IN LOVE: Dermot McArdle and
Kelly Ann Corcoran on their wedding day, and
(right) Kelly Ann with one of her young kids

LONG WAIT FOR JUSTICE: *Star* reporter
Michael O'Toole talks to Kelly Ann's dad Ted Cor-
coran and sister Caroline Moran. (Below) Kelly
Ann's dad Ted and her brother Ted junior watch
Dermot McArdle as he leaves Malaga court

GUILTY: McArdle leaves
Dundalk District Court after
his conviction for assault

LYNSEY O'BRIEN:
Dream cruise turns to nightmare

I T WAS meant to be a dream holiday. The O'Brien family from Dublin had travelled to the United States for a post-Christmas break. A week in sun-drenched Florida was to be followed by a Caribbean cruise. No expense had been spared and the wealthy family, who had struck it rich during the boom years, planned on enjoying themselves.

But days into the trip, disaster struck when 15-year-old Lynsey fell overboard after bingeing on a concoction of alcoholic drinks. Despite frantic attempts to rescue the teenager, her body was lost to the ocean. It is a nightmare her family have never woken up from.

"In the blink of an eye, our whole world was turned upside down. Nothing has ever been the same since," explained Lynsey's mother, Sandra O'Brien. "Our family has been torn apart, to lose a child like that, there is no going back. You don't ever get over it."

Lynsey was a typical teenager, obsessed with fashion, her school friends and boys. The pretty Dubliner was the second-eldest child, and incredibly close to mum, Sandra, and dad, Paul. Her death in 2006 off the coast of Mexico devastated her family, tore the parents' marriage apart, and left a void in the O'Brien household that can never be filled.

Such an indiscriminate disaster was never intended to be a part of the O'Brien family's script.

Self-made millionaires, Paul and Sandra had created a life of luxury for themselves and their children. Both from modest backgrounds, they had become the epitome of the Celtic Tiger success story with a property portfolio that afforded them a millionaire lifestyle.

"We had it all. New cars every year, holidays. A big house," explained Sandra. "We were always lucky when it came to business. Things happened for us. But we never let the success go to our heads or change us. We weren't that type."

As 2005 came to a close, the O'Briens were riding the crest of a wave. With a number of rental properties in and around Dublin and stakes in two factories, money was no object.

They lived in a mansion in leafy Terenure in Dublin and their four children, Kelly, Lynsey, Imelda, and Dean, wanted for nothing, attending top fee-paying schools.

As a treat to ring in the New Year, Paul and Sandra decided to take the family on a dream trip to the States.

They had friends living in Florida and, together with a group of pals from Dublin, had organised to spend a week in the Sunshine State followed by a seven-night luxury cruise. It was to be a reunion of sorts as the old friends had not been together as a group for 25 years.

"There were 22 of us in all who went on the cruise, including parents and kids. The holiday had been going so well up to that point. We had had a great time in Florida and everyone was getting on really well," remembers Sandra.

The group boarded the plush *Costa Magica* cruise liner on New Year's Day in Fort Lauderdale.

Part of the Italian-based Costa Cruise Line group, the *Costa Magica* was built in 2004 and is one of the company's largest liners. Italian-themed, it boasts 13 decks and can accommodate 2,720 guests. From the moment guests step on board, they are waited on by the ships staff, and it didn't take Lynsey and her friends long to get to grips with life onboard the ship of dreams.

Dream cruise turns to nightmare

"It was a dream holiday really. The gang we were with were all good friends and the kids all knew each other and got on. We had no fears about letting the teenagers go off and explore. Some of the group had young children with them, if we were worried about anyone it was the younger kids," said Sandra.

From sampling the nightly entertainment, to shopping, to sunbathing, Lynsey was enjoying the holiday of a lifetime. But on the third night of the cruise, the fun came to an abrupt and shocking end.

The evening had started pleasantly with the group going for a meal together in one of the ship's four plush restaurants.

The adults sat at one table, while the teenagers gathered at another. Sandra remembers Lynsey did not eat much on that occasion.

"She was a thin build and her appetite was never the best. I don't think she ate much at all that night, none of the kids did, but that's kids for you. We would probably have got them room service later if they were hungry. They were excited to be on the ship and were having fun," she said.

As the night wore on, Lynsey and a female pal slipped away from the restaurant. Unbeknownst to their parents, they were planning on doing some partying of their own and had sought out a quieter pub some decks below. Lynsey found the most secluded bar on board and — according to receipts — drank as much as she could in an alarmingly short space of time.

Between 10.27pm of January 4 and 12.09am of January 5, Lynsey ordered eight drinks — some of them were for her pal, but most of them she knocked back herself, even using a straw to maximise the effects of the alcohol.

The list of liquor served to the 15-year-old was frightening. It included two Sex On The Beach drinks, three Woo Woos, both of which are strong vodka and peach Schnapps-based cocktails.

On top of that she downed two vodka mixers and an extra shot of vodka, which was on the house.

Such a volume of alcohol would be enough to leave a

seasoned drinker feeling the worse for wear. For a teenager who was still at the point of experimenting, the binge had devastating consequences.

At around midnight, Sandra — noticing that her daughter had been gone for quite some time — dispatched her eldest daughter Kelly, who was 16 at the time, to locate her younger sister. The former hairdresser recalls getting a sense that all was not right.

"You know that feeling you get when you don't see the kids for a while, you start to wonder where they are and what they are up to, so Kelly went off and got them. When she brought Lynsey back up to us, we knew she was drunk. She didn't speak, but I knew she was," Sandra recalled.

"I wasn't happy at all about it because she was 15 and to have drunk so much on a boat where we thought the legal age was 21, well, let's just say, both Paul and myself planned to have words the following morning with the management.

"For the whole time we were in America, we knew they wouldn't get served as it is so strict there. And there was nothing around the ships to say it was any different. We believed it would be as strict. I was angry, but more because I thought she would have been safe on that ship, and not able to go down and buy a whole rake of cocktails."

With Lynsey safely back, Paul and Sandra decided to call it a night, and the family retired to their interconnecting cabins at around 2am.

"Paul brought us all up to the room," Sandra said. "I was in with Lynsey in her and Imelda's room. We had put her to bed. Our room was through a set of doors. We always did that when we were away, have the kids bedrooms connected to our own. I remember telling Lynsey we would deal with it tomorrow and Paul gave her a kiss. I walked back into our own room with Paul, and Kelly was ringing room service. Then I heard the screams."

Moments after her parents had left her, Lynsey had stumbled out of bed and opened the door which led onto the seventh-floor balcony.

Needing to be sick, her parents believe she pushed a chair up against the glass railings. Clearly still feeling the effects of the alcohol, she lost her footing and fell 140ft into the sea. Her younger sister, Imelda, who was only 12 at the time, was the first to spot that her sister was in difficulty.

She began screaming and tried to open the door to the balcony.

"Imelda could see Lynsey going over the railing. She was screaming trying to get out to her. Then Lynsey fell and all hell broke loose," remembers Sandra.

One floor above the O'Briens, Kurt Byrd and his wife, Sharon, both veteran police officers with the Cincinnati Police Department in the United States, heard the same scream and reacted quickly — running to the ship's balcony.

"I immediately told Sharon. I said, start looking in the water, start looking in the water," said Mr Byrd. "And we went right to the edge of the balcony and started looking over, and we didn't see anything."

While his wife was searching the water for a body, Byrd raced to the phone and called the emergency number. He told the operator something was very wrong downstairs.

"We heard a thump, we heard a terrible scream," Byrd recalled telling the operator. "Something's going on in the room directly below us. You need to get somebody up here."

The cruise liner's alarm was sounded and news quickly spread someone had gone overboard.

Completely distraught, Paul remembers charging all over the ship, looking for help. "I was banging on walls, I was screaming, I was frantic. I was in shock. ... I was totally, totally, I can't describe how I felt," he said.

"People were running everywhere," recalls Sandra. "It was panic. One man was throwing life rings in after Lynsey and letting off flares. Poor Paul wanted to jump in after her. But it was dark and we were out in the middle of the sea."

Given the size of the ship, it took almost 15 minutes to slow the boat down to an adequate speed in order to turn back around.

Mr Byrd, who was a commander of an underwater search and rescue unit, claimed that it took too long before anyone threw a life ring. By the time the boat did turn around to start the search, he said he called the emergency number again to complain about the search.

"I said unless this girl's an Olympic swimmer, she's not going to make it anywhere to these life rings," he said. "She's three to five-plus miles away from this boat, and she's not going to make it to here. You're searching in the wrong area. In my department, if we handled an investigation this way, we'd be fired."

The Byrds later went on US prime-time television and were highly critical of the attempts to save Lynsey.

"The way they handled the situation, they failed, totally. And they failed Lynsey," Sharon said.

Despite all the efforts to save Lynsey, it was too late. In fact, her mother said that even if the ship had been able to stop sooner, her daughter would still have lost her life — as she believes Lynsey hit her head off a lifeboat as she fell and was unconscious as she impacted the water. In ways, such a quick death is a comfort to her.

"They brought us all down to a room that night and I remember saying to my friends to go and check and see was Lynsey hiding behind the bed, I just couldn't believe it was after happening," Sandra added.

"Poor Paul didn't believe it either. But now I think she was dead before she even hit the water. I wouldn't like to think that she was in the water and was aware of what was happening, the ship still moving away, that would be too awful."

In the direct aftermath of the tragedy, the O'Brien family's shock quickly turned to anger. Appalled that their 15-year-old daughter could have been served such a lethal amount of booze, they demanded answers.

Both parents firmly believe Lynsey would not have lost her life if she had been refused service in the ship's bar.

"Just look at the concoction of the stuff she was served. Vodkas and cocktails, I mean, I don't drink that type of stuff, no-one I know drinks that kind of stuff," Sandra said.

"She couldn't handle that. The pal she was drinking with actually got sick, if Lynsey had got sick it would have been a different story."

Devoted dad Paul is of the same view. "She was in an in-toxicated state," he said. "I had just kissed her goodnight and left the room not 60 seconds when I heard the screams. In that time, she must have gone out to the balcony to be sick and accidentally fell in."

As attention turned to the barman who served Lynsey, another version of events emerged.

Barman Earle Moulton claimed that Lynsey had produced a fake ID which stated that she was 23.

In a controversial interview given after the schoolgirl's death, he claimed Lynsey appeared to be an experienced drinker, despite her young age. "As a barman you can tell: some people can handle a lot of drink and some people can't. You could tell straight away that Lynsey drank a lot," he said.

Receipts obtained after Lynsey's death show she had been served at least eight alcoholic drinks onboard, despite being under-age.

Moulton said Lynsey was a fiery character, had shown him convincing ID and had insisted she was two years over the American legal age of drinking.

In a further display of immense insensitivity, he also claimed Lynsey had jumped to her own death after arguing with her parents.

"Lynsey had been sent to her cabin and she was very unhappy about it. I heard this from other people on the ship and it was in the report that was filed by security. She commit-ted suicide, there was something wrong with her," he said.

Reports also emerged that Lynsey was spotted swing-ing from the railings and security had to be called after a disturbance at her cabin.

Such comments pierced the schoolgirl's parents' hearts. They have rubbished all of these claims and absolutely refute suggestions that their daughter took her own life.

Paul is adamant that his daughter was incapable of even comprehending such an act. "She loved her life, she was happy and had no reason to do that. Suicide has not crossed my mind for a minute. I know she did not kill herself," he insisted.

Such a suggestion is also inconceivable to Sandra. "Suicide? She had too much to live for, she wasn't depressed, she was a teenager, who had her humours every now and then. Show me a teenager that doesn't. But there was nothing wrong with Lynsey that night other than she was drunk because she was served such an insane amount of drink," Sandra said.

"I know my daughter. She was in love with life. I was with her on New Year's Eve shopping to bring presents home for her boyfriend and her friends. She would never have dreamed of going out onto to that balcony and doing something like that, no way."

Sandra is also convinced that her daughter did not produce a fake ID. "I don't believe that for a second. She didn't try anything like that in Florida. And even if she did, Lynsey was 15, she looked 15, she sounded like a 15-year-old. There was no way in hell she would have passed for 23 years of age. No way."

In the harrowing days that followed, the O'Brien family did not disembark the *Costa Magica* and stayed on board the cruise ship until its return four days later to Fort Lauderdale.

They chose to do this as they did not want to get off in Mexico and fly home from there and also did not want to leave while the search for Lynsey's remains was ongoing.

Over the course of those days a memorial service was held on the ship for Lynsey.

Flower petals were thrown into the ocean and prayers were said. In Ireland, school pals of Lynsey, who was a transition-year student at Loreto High School Beaufort in Rathfarnham, comforted each other. A Mass was held and counselling services were made available to shocked students.

The school's chairman John Phelan said at the time: "The guidance counsellor has been with many of the students this morning because, as you can imagine, many are very upset. Everybody is absolutely devastated. Many of the pupils who knew her would be very young, about 15 or 16, and we need to give them as much support as they need. Our main concern is for the students and their families at this very hard time."

He added that Lynsey was a "very vibrant, popular girl"

Behind the scenes, anger was continuing to brew.

Lynsey's parents were now intent on getting justice for their daughter and looked into hiring an international maritime lawyer, Brett Rivkind.

The experienced lawyer responded by saying he was confident the O'Briens had a case against the cruise operator.

Arriving back in Ireland, the O'Briens slowly began to come to terms with their loss, as a titanic war of words erupted across the Atlantic.

The complexities of the legal system which operates at sea quickly became clear. One of the biggest dangers on board cruise ships is the fact that they are "in a sense, lawless".

The O'Briens' lawyer Mr Rivkind explained: "There is no clear-cut definition to whose laws apply. For example, in this case you have an Irish citizen on board a ship sailing under an Italian flag in Mexican waters. There are different procedures in every case. There is no definition as to whose laws apply and it takes some time to find out."

But the top lawyer insisted the bald fact was that Lynsey's death was directly related to alcohol consumption.

In the weeks that followed, barman Earle Moulton was sacked by the cruise operator for what they claimed was failure to inspect Lynsey's alleged ID closely enough. Costa Cruise Line also said that it had implemented alcohol education for other staff.

The media was not slow in taking ownership of the tragedy and the O'Briens found themselves in the eye of an storm.

Every word they uttered became headline news in Ireland and the United States. "It was a really big thing," said Sandra. "I don't think it was just because Lynsey died, but also because we were seen as a wealthy family, it happened on a cruise ship. It was like it had everything for the newspapers."

As the row over Lynsey's under-age drinking continued, speculation about a multi-million compensation package intensified.

But the cruise line company responded with a statement stating that media reports made by the O'Brien family and their representatives regarding the circumstances surrounding this tragedy were incorrect and misleading, adding "there is no evidence suggesting an accidental fall".

Four months after Lynsey's death, the cruise firm finally released the findings of their own investigation.

They claimed that there was no evidence to support the claim that Lynsey had fallen overboard by accident. In its report into the tragedy, the cruise firm also insisted it was not guilty of any wrongdoing surrounding the death.

The hard-hitting report stated:
●There was no evidence suggesting an accidental fall.
●Lynsey and a friend ordered four or five drinks each over a two-hour period.
●Lynsey showed ID to a bartender stating she was 23 years old.
●The teenager's last purchase from the bar occurred almost two hours before she was reported overboard.

The company concluded that Lynsey's death was caused by "underage drinking". The cruise firm also claimed there had been many "false and misleading" reports about the circumstances surrounding her death.

The owners of the *Costa Magica* said they continued to extend their deepest sympathies to the devastated family. But they claimed their report cleared them of any wrongdoing.

"The results of Costa's analysis clearly indicate that the issue at hand is underage drinking," a spokeswoman said.

Dream cruise turns to nightmare

The spokeswoman also pointed out that, although the ship is not legally required to maintain a minimum drinking age of 21 while at sea, they voluntarily enforce the age limit.

The report found: "In violation of this policy, Lynsey O'Brien, along with another guest, ordered, purchased and were served a total of four or five drinks each, which they consumed over an approximately two-hour period.

"Lynsey is reported to have shown identification to a bartender indicating she was 23 years of age. The bartender stopped serving Lynsey alcohol after being informed she was not 21 years of age. He was subsequently fired for failing to properly scrutinise her identification."

Despite these findings, loving mum Sandra continues to lay the blame for her daughter's death squarely on the fact that she was served alcohol when she should not have been.

"I know for a fact that if Lynsey had not been served drink then Lynsey would still be here with us today and life would not have gone the way it has for my family. I was there, I know what happened," she said.

A confidential compensation package was later agreed between the two parties.

The attention that came with Lynsey's death shone a spotlight on the billion-dollar cruise industry and exposed to an Irish audience, for the first time, some of the stark realities behind the fun-in-the-sun image.

Between 2003 and 2005 alone, cruise industry figures show 24 passengers and four crew members disappeared from cruise ships. There have also been countless cases of rape, mysterious disappearances, theft, and assault all around the globe.

One of the most disturbing cases was that of honeymooner, George Smith, who vanished from his cruise ship *The Brilliance of the Seas*, which is part of the Royal Caribbean fleet, a few months before Lynsey's death in 2006.

Slain Abroad

The American man's disappearance was initially dismissed as an accident or suicide, despite signs suggesting foul play.

The missing man's family refused to accept this version of events and pressed for an investigation.

Among the dramatic elements that later emerged was a giant bloodstain which was found below his balcony.

In the hours before he disappeared he was known to have drank absinthe, which may cause hallucinations, and a few days after he vanished some of his drinking buddies were thrown off the boat after a female passenger accused them of rape. Compensation in excess of $1m was eventually paid to his family by the cruise liner.

Then there was the high-profile case of US businesswoman Janet Kelly who was sexually assaulted by a barman during a cruise from southern California to Mexico (a confidentiality order prohibits the mention of the cruise lines or cruise ship).

On the last day of her cruise in 2000 she stopped at a poolside bar before dinner. The bartender, who in the days prior had been friendly but not overly flirtatious, handed her a fruity concoction that had an unwanted kick.

Kelly, who is convinced that the drink was drugged, said she felt her legs go rubbery and her mind turn to mush as the bartender led her to an employees-only restroom and raped her before she passed out cold.

After flying home the next day, she went to a hospital and was tested for evidence of sexual assault.

The FBI, which is the lead agency for investigating incidents involving US citizens on the high seas, took several weeks to interview the bartender, who claimed what happened in that bathroom stall had been consensual.

Kelly sued the cruise line, which promptly fired the bartender for misconduct and sent him home to Jamaica.

Several months later, she discovered through private investigators that he had been hired by another cruise line. She eventually settled a lawsuit with the company in question.

In response to these and other cases, the International Cruise Victims Organization (ICV) was set up. With several hundred members, the group represents victims of crime on cruise ships, their families and friends, and individuals concerned about the problems of victimisation and disappearances on cruise ships.

In the wake of Lynsey's high-profile death, intense lobbying by the group led to the setting up of US congressional hearings into the issue of crimes on cruise ships.

Particular attention was given to passenger disappearances and sexual assaults. ICV is led by Ken Carver, whose daughter Merrian Carver disappeared from the Celebrity cruise ship.

In that case, Ms Carver's cabin attendant testified that when he reported his suspicion that she was no longer aboard three days into the voyage, he was told to keep putting fresh chocolates on her pillow. At the end of the trip, his supervisor placed Ms Carver's belongings in storage without notifying her family or the authorities.

Sandra got in touch with ICV after Lynsey's death and found their support helpful. "It was good to have someone to talk to who has been through something similar. I think they have done really good work," she said.

Efforts by the group would eventually lead the US government to introduce new legislation, the Cruise Vessel Security and Safety Act of 2010.

The new laws, signed by President Barack Obama, introduced wide-ranging new rules for any ship sailing to or from the US, including an order that ship rails must be at least 42 inches high, video surveillance equipment must be installed to monitor passenger safety and "passenger overboard" situations, and the establishment of acoustic hailing or warning devices that can be heard throughout the ship — for alerting passengers to danger — must be overseen.

Provision was also made to ensure that, should a sexual assault occur on board a cruise ship, the victim has access to trained first responders and to a confidential means of communication with law enforcement, legal and victim advocacy professionals.

Would any of this have helped to save Lynsey's life? Her

still grieving mother is unsure.

"Higher railings are a good idea, but honestly I would prefer to see balconies covered in glass. I was afraid to go on the balcony during our cruise and I wouldn't let my son, Dean, out there. But in Lynseys case I just feel if she had not have been served drink she would still be alive, it is as simple as that," she reiterated.

While happy that future passengers will now be safer, Sandra can't help but wonder why her own daughter had to be taken away from her family in such cruel circumstances, the pain of which continues to be inflicted on her family.

On the first anniversary of Lynsey's death, her younger sister Imelda, now aged 17, wrote a heart-breaking message to her lost sibling on the social networking site, Bebo, revealing for the first time the horror that she witnessed on that fateful January night.

"Me and Kelly ordered food and Dad gave you a kiss good-night and Mum put the latch on the balcony door. Then they left the room and I saw you hanging over the side and I couldn't get the door opened and when I did I saw you fall and hit your head and hit the water."

The Bebo page became a shrine to Lynsey with almost 70,000 hits logged after the teenager's death.

One close friend wrote: "I miss all your advice, I keep thinking you're coming back, I still don't understand why you had to go."

Sandra said her three surviving children, Kelly, now 22, Imelda, and Dean, now aged 13, struggled to accept what has happened to their sister.

"There was a lot of anger, it was very hard for them. It was very hard for us all. The months after Lynsey died it felt like I was having a heart attack that never ended," Sandra explained.

Dream cruise turns to nightmare

The stress and anguish of losing a child also heavily impacted on Paul and Sandra's marriage.

The couple were teenage sweethearts and married when they were in their early 20s. But 12 months after losing Lynsey, they separated.

"I didn't just lose my daughter, I lost my husband and my family was torn apart. I am living a nightmare, one that never ends," Sandra said.

"Losing Lynsey, it broke us all. Paul and I separated about a year after she died. It was just so much to take. We had our ups and downs like any marriage, but if Lynsey hadn't been taken from us then I don't think we would be where we are now.

"It was a nightmare, it still haunts us all. Every night, I don't sleep properly. I don't think we will ever accept it. "

The recession gripped Ireland in 2008, and also devastated the couple's finances.

"Sometimes I wake up in the morning and I wonder how I will keep going, I wonder what happened to my life," she admitted.

"How did it all go so wrong? It is worse than a disaster movie. I am living a nightmare. Some days I might get up and some days I don't. I am not depressed, I just can't see how my life went so wrong.

"I have lost my husband, my family has been broken up, I lost my daughter and I almost lost everything else. The recession has destroyed our businesses.

"But money and everything — none of it means anything to me anymore. People are losing their houses and they are devastated, but what is more devastating than losing a child?"

However the devoted mother continues to struggle on and hopes that one day the immense pain of losing Lynsey might lessen and the dark clouds that settled over her family the night Lynsey lost her life so tragically might, one day, be replaced once again by blue skies.

"They say time is a great healer, don't they? I'm not sure about that, I can't see how we will ever get over losing

Lynsey," Sandra added. "Things will never go back to normal, but I suppose I hope in the future the hurt won't be so bad for us all. I know Lynsey is looking down on us and I am sure she hopes for that too."

IRISH KILLED ON 9/11:
The death towers

IT WAS a perfect morning. As New Yorkers streamed into work, the blue skies overhead promised another glorious day of late summer sunshine. But at exactly 8.46am hell came calling to the Big Apple — and over the following 102 minutes the face of America would be changed forever.

The 11th of September 2001 should have been just another Tuesday morning, but it would go down as a day of infamy when a hijacked airliner, American Airlines Flight 11 flying out of Boston, crashed into the North Tower of the World Trade Center at 470mph with 10,000 gallons of fuel onboard.

Seventeen minutes later another hijacked plane, United Airlines Flight 175 flying from Logan airport in Boston to Los Angeles, slammed into the South Tower.

The United States of America was under attack and the situation was quickly spiralling out of control. Reports emerged that two more planes had been taken over by Muslim fanatics. One was en route to the symbol of the US military, the Pentagon in Virginia. The other would never reach its destination after passengers fought back against their captors, helping to crash the plane near Shanksville, Pennsylvania.

At home in Ireland it was lunchtime, and the nation watched in horror as pictures emerged of fireballs engulfing the World

Trade Center. The world was shocked by images of terrified men and women caught in the top floors, committing suicide by jumping from the towers before they collapsed.

Worried relatives instantly thought of loved ones living and working in New York. Ireland's links with the famous city have been forged over the centuries. From the hundreds of thousands who arrived on coffin ships to escape the famine of the 1840s to the more recent exodus fleeing economic hardship, New York has always been a haven for the Irish. They in turn left their mark on the city — building the skyscrapers, policing the streets and eventually running City Hall.

But as the horror of 9/11 unfolded, it quickly became clear that mass casualties were inevitable — and it was only a matter of time before Irish deaths emerged. In the days that followed it became apparent that virtually no county in Ireland would be left untouched as the names of emigrants and Irish Americans appeared on the growing list of dead.

Each person named as missing or dead had their own tragic story to tell.

Early on that fateful September morning, at Boston's Logan Airport, 44-year-old businesswoman Ruth McCourt was waiting with her four-year-old daughter Juliana.

Originally from Ballintemple, Co Cork, Ruth had moved to America in 1973 as a teenager and thrived in the land of opportunity, eventually setting up her own beauty business in Boston. Mother and daughter were going on a vacation to LA and had been on standby since earlier that morning. They were delighted when they were eventually allocated seats along with 54 fellow passenger aboard United Airlines Flight 175.

Ruth had been planning the special treat for her only daughter, nicknamed Miss J, for months. It was every young girl's dream — a trip to Disneyland — and mother and daughter were in high spirits as they took their seats on the morning flight. With Ruth's striking red hair and her daughter's curly blonde locks they would have been quite the pair. Juliana was only four, but already displayed a sense of wit and personality. Ruth's mother Paula Clifford Scott said mother and daughter were incredibly close. "She was a nurturer like her mother."

Ruth's best friend Paige Farley-Hackel (46) was also going on the holiday. Close as sisters, the pair had become pals at the day spa Ruth used to own in Boston. When she married David McCourt in 1995, Ruth gave up the business and became a homemaker and later a devoted mother to her only child, but her friendship with Paige lasted, and they shared a passion for reading, cooking and learning new things.

They met that morning in Boston Airport and were due to fly together — but when Ms Farley-Hackel realised she could use frequent flyer miles, she got a ticket for American Airlines Flight 11 instead.

Shortly after takeoff, Flight 175 was yanked from its flight path by hijackers. Minutes earlier, the plane carrying Ms Farley-Hackel had also been taken over by terrorists and turned into a missile, crashing into the North Tower of the World Trade Center and killing everyone on board.

As Ruth's plane hurtled towards Lower Manhattan and to certain death, she could never have known that fate had placed her brother Ronnie at a meeting in the very same skyscraper where she and her daughter would meet their fiery end.

Ronnie Clifford (56) had followed his sister to the United States in 1980 and made a life for himself, marrying and buying a house in New Jersey. The computer software businessman was staying at the Marriott World Trade Center Hotel on the day of the attack. He was minutes from attending a meeting at the North Tower when disaster struck.

"I felt the impact of the first plane crash in a hotel at the foot of one of the towers," Ronnie recalled. "It is still hard to explain the sensation, but your instincts just kick in. You just want to survive. It was my daughter's birthday that day and that was in my mind, to get home to her and my family."

After running outside, he recalled how he was confronted

by a badly-burned woman, barely recognisable due to the extent of her injuries.

"Out of the haze came this shadow of a woman, very badly burned. After helping her we heard the second explosion, which rocked the whole building. Then pieces were falling everywhere."

Despite the risk to his own safety, the proud Irishman helped the woman, 40-year-old Jennie Ann Maffeo, to an ambulance. "I guided Jennie Ann to helping hands, through a street littered with the remains from planes used as missiles to attack New York City," he said. "She was burned over 90 per cent of her body and died 40 days later.

"On that day, at the base of the Twin Towers, I saw death, I smelt death, I heard death, and I have relived these deaths daily since that morning."

Ronnie, along with thousands of others, managed to flee the burning North Tower. He was fortunate that he did as the iconic building was in its death throes.

The end came at 10.28am, when the 110-storey tower imploded floor by floor, spewing out clouds of debris and atomised flesh. As he watched from a distance Ronnie could never have realised that in the clear blue sky above him, his sister and his niece had also been sent to their deaths.

"I felt the shudder of the second plane striking the North Tower — the plane that carried my sister and niece. As I struggled for my own life on the ground below, Ruth and Juliana were meant to be on their way to Disneyland. To think that I managed to escape something like that but that my sister and her young daughter would lose their life, it still doesn't seem possible."

An hour later Ronnie was informed by his family that his sister and her daughter had been on board one of the doomed planes. In the weeks and months to come, Ronnie said he tried to imagine what their final moments would have been like.

"I've tried to imagine Ruth's last moments. Sitting next to Juliana and calming her, knowing there was terrorist activity going on in the plane and leaning into her — maybe singing her a lullaby and helping to calm the people around her. She was a fantastic mother."

Ruth and Juliana's death devastated their loved ones — and 10 years on the pain of their loss is still hard to take. To this day Ronnie says he cannot face returning to Ground Zero.

"I witnessed the annihilation firsthand. I cope on a day-to-day basis. I've moved on — it has made me more spiritual — but we still miss Ruth, really miss her. My sister was my great friend. She was a lot of fun. It's a huge void that will never be filled. I drive past Ground Zero, but I don't go back there."

Another of Ruth's brothers, Mark Clifford (51), still lives in Co Cork. He said that for many years afterwards watching footage of the attacks felt like he was watching "a trailer from a movie".

"It is very difficult to look at the replays of the planes hitting the towers," Mark said. "I still think it is one of the most surreal events in my life. Ruth was a magical person. She was very special. We remember Ruth and Juliana with love and affection. It is very sad to see these people with so much to give, no longer with us. Time helps heal the pain but it never goes, not really."

Some months after the event, a headstone was erected in memory of Ruth and Juliana in St Finbarr's Cemetery in Cork. Family members, including Ruth's eldest brother John (57), scattered their ashes at the graves of Ruth's father Val and her brother Gordon.

Mark, who runs a security firm in Cork, said his sister always had a great love for her native country, and added that it was important to mark her passing on native soil.

"We had a lovely, quiet and dignified service for Ruth," he said. "She always had a strong desire to return to Ireland. She had plans for a holiday home here. We were very glad that Ruth's remains were brought home."

Ruth's heartbroken husband David set up a special children's education fund dedicated to the memory of his beloved daughter. David said he set up the fund because he wanted to have a permanent memorial for his "loving and giving child".

"Juliana was an extraordinary example of a person who displayed sensitivity to everyone's feelings. If we can pass that gift on, to create more harmony among children, future generations will be more compassionate. Juliana will have given the greatest spiritual gift," he said.

Despite their horrific loss, Ruth's family were among the fortunate few who were able to bury their loved one. Many who lost family on that fateful day in September have never received a body to bury This was something, which in the dark months after the catastrophe, made grieving all the harder.

AnneMarie McHugh had been at her desk inside Tower Two early on the morning of 9/11. When not working for the EuroBrokers firm, the 35-year-old stockbroker from Tuam, Co Galway, was busy planning her wedding, a month away.

Her fiancee Patrick Day said the very first minute he saw the Irish woman with the long red hair and clear blue eyes, he knew he had met the woman he was going to marry.

"I remember kissing her cheek and getting that exact feeling," Patrick said. "She was just perfect for me and I was perfect for her. We were honest with each other, we were good to each other."

Born on March 17 of Irish-American stock in South Dakota, Patrick said the memory of his last weekend with AnneMarie will never leave him. On the Friday, AnneMarie had bought tickets for Patrick to see the Yankees.

"The tickets were so good I remember kissing her and saying this is baseball paradise," he said.

On the Saturday they stayed in their apartment, playing games on the PlayStation and watching science fiction programmes on TV. Sunday was the All-Ireland final. AnneMarie visited her parents Padraig and Margaret, who used to run a pub in Tuam, a few times each year and she was an avid supporter of the GAA. Born in New York, her family had moved to Galway when she was a young girl and she went to school in Tuam and later attended University College Galway.

"Galway lost — but it was a great day anyway," remembered Patrick.

On the Monday, Patrick met up with his friend and they planned a small bachelor party for that night. AnneMarie and Patrick were due to get married in Florence the following November, and planned to start a family immediately.

"We had picked the names, John Patrick for the first boy, Katie for the first girl. We were both so excited," he said.

AnneMarie wasn't feeling well on Monday night, so she stayed home while Patrick went to watch the first game of the football season. It rained out and so he went for a drink with a friend instead. When he got home, Anne was still awake.

"We talked for a couple of hours. I wasn't feeling too good because of all the hotdogs I'd eaten and neither of us could sleep," he said. Eventually they slept, and Patrick said he woke a few times in the night to find AnneMarie's hand in his.

"We always cuddled up together but it was unusual for us to be holding hands. I thought a lot about that afterwards."

The alarm didn't go off that morning. Patrick remembers thinking AnneMarie might skip work that day — they could go out for lunch and she could finish writing the wedding invitations. But AnneMarie got up, took a shower, and Patrick walked her to the door.

"I can see her by the elevator, laughing at me, saying be a good boy now and call me when you get to work," he said.

He walked to the New York Public Library where he worked designing museum exhibits. As soon as he arrived he called AnneMarie in her office on the 89th floor.

They chatted for around half an hour until she told him: "Something's hit the building, I gotta go."

AnneMarie had been in the World Trade Center when the bomb went off in 1993. Then, she had walked down 107 flights of stairs to safety.

"I fully expected to see her walking down the street covered in dust, I wouldn't eat because I wanted to wait for her,'

Patrick said. "I wouldn't even have a cup of coffee. I just kept saying I'll eat and drink with Annie when she comes home."

AnneMarie was last seen on the 40th floor as she tried to escape. Her body has never been recovered.

Family friend Paddy Talty, secretary of Tuam Stadium Development, revealed that the proud Galway woman, who was wearing the county jersey on the day she lost her life, is believed to have stopped to help some stranded workers.

"Apparently she wore the jersey every day and was wearing it on 9/11," Paddy said. "We heard after how she was coming down the stairs with some of her work pals, but she stopped to help a group who were trapped in an office.

"By all accounts her pals urged her to leave with them. I believe they got out alive, but Anne stayed to try and help and that was the last that was seen of her."

Patrick said the loss of his soulmate broke his heart. "I think about Anne every day, I cry because I miss her. But I am so glad for what we had together. But so angry too. At least one thing I know is that she never spent one day without knowing I loved her. Nothing was ever left unsaid or undemonstrated.

"To be honest Anne was the only girl for me. She loved soccer, she got the soccer package on the TV so we could watch football. She loved science fiction, football and PlayStation — she was the perfect woman.

"I don't feel as lonely as I did before I met her. I wouldn't dare forget her and I just think I'm so lucky to have had that time with her. That doesn't mean I don't feel cheated or angry because I do — but you can't complain about what you don't get because that just ruins what you had."

Patrick also said the pain of never getting AnneMarie's remains back in order to have a funeral made the grieving process all the harder for him. "Because her remains were never found there was no defining moment when I was told she wasn't coming back. Eventually I just had to give up hope that she was going to get out of there all right," he said. "She should have lived but she must have been helping people.

"I try not to think about where she was when she died. But

every time I get into an elevator or climb a stairwell in the city I wonder.

"The hardest thing for me is coming home to an empty apartment. We couldn't bear to be away from each other. Sometimes I hear myself saying things she would have said."

Patrick still wears a Celtic gold ring on his wedding finger which the couple picked together. Inscribed on it are the words Always and Forever in Irish. "It makes me happy to wear my wedding ring. It reminds me of the time we had together."

The Coughlan family pub in the quaint village of Cappawhite in Co Tipperary displays a poster of the World Trade Center — a sign that the horror of September 11 broke hearts in the Premier County too.

Beneath the poster is a plaque reading: "In memory of Martin Coughlan: Journeyman, Carpenter, Trade Unionist." They are reminders of the boy born in an upstairs bedroom, who perished in the Twin Towers attack at the age of 53.

As a youngster, Martin's favorite game was cowboys and Indians and as a teen he idolized Elvis and longed to visit Graceland. In his late 30s, having worked in England, he finally acted on his dream of traveling to America.

With his wife Catherine, the talented carpenter travelled to New York, to build his dream life. He immediately set about finding work in the construction trade to provide for his wife and four daughters, Orla, Ailish, Sinead and Denise. His brother Patrick explained: "He came back to Ireland regularly but New York was his home. He thought it was an exciting place to live."

Shortly after they came to New York in 1987, Catherine told her husband that she did not want the family to live in an apartment. Martin responded by zealously pursuing jobs, often working seven days a week so that the family could move into a house in Bayside, Queens. "He just wanted a comfortable home and a car that worked and to see that we were educated," said his eldest daughter Orla Bowie.

Niece Linda Coughlan recalled: "He worked six, seven days a week to put the girls through college. He might be going off to work at 6am just as we were coming home from a night out." Linda spent the summer of 1998 with her relatives. "They were all Daddy's girls," she said. "They might spend two hours at the dinner table, talking through their days."

Martin's job with the Sweeney and Heekin Carpentry and Dry Wall Corporation of Long Island City took him to buildings all around Manhattan — and on September 10 and 11 2001, he found himself working at the World Trade Center.

Back home on the morning of September 11, Martin's native village was getting ready to celebrate. The county hurling team had won the All-Ireland championship that weekend, and two villagers on the team were returning home as conquering heroes. From across the Atlantic, Martin phoned his best friend baker, Austin Buckley, to share in the excitement.

"He was sorry be couldn't be there," Buckley recalled. "But he was still working two carpentry jobs in New York and was heading to his favorite workplace, the World Trade Center. He was so, so proud of working in the Twin Towers. When I was over there earlier in the year, he took me through the building showing me all his projects — a window here, a wall there."

Moments after the first plane struck, Martin phoned this wife from the 89th floor of the South Tower to reassure her that he was safe. An answering machine picked up his message.

"There's been a bomb in the building, but I'm OK, and tell the four girls I'll be home for dinner."

In a second message, sounding fearful and fighting for breath from running or smoke, Martin said he was trying to escape from the building and was headed for the lifts.

Back in the family pub, Martin's sister-in-law Josie was behind the bar. She had two brothers who ran Manhattan pubs, a son with two kids in Yonkers, and a son-in-law on Wall Street. She hadn't known Martin did jobs in the World Trade Center and was more concerned that one of Martin's four daughters might be caught in the area.

"There was a lot of worry,' Josie said. "All that day we were waiting for the phone to ring to find out what was happening. We said a lot of prayers.'

Eventually, all the far-flung Coughlans called in to say they were OK — everyone except Martin. Two weeks later, rescuers found Martin's body with his wallet intact.

"I knew he was dead," best pal Austin Buckley said. "But I spent two weeks in my chair watching the TV news, hoping to see him come running out of the rubble and the smoke. I felt like a zombie by the end. What a morbid time."

The death of the devoted husband and father shattered his family, impacting particularly hard on his wife Catherine. After a lifetime of hard work, she had been looking forward to spending her golden years with her husband. He had earned a pension and was thinking of coming home to Ireland.

"I was finally getting him to relax on Sundays," Catherine said. "We were just getting our life back. The pain of it never leaves, it is there every day. We miss him just as much."

In a poignant online tribute to her father, Martin's daughter Denise wrote: "Martin John Coughlan was my father. But he wasn't just my father because I just so happened to be born.

"He was my father because he cared about me. Raised me. Loved me. Picked me up from dance class never being a second late. Encouraged me. Gave me someone to look up to. Made me laugh. Gave me everything I ever needed, even when I didn't deserve it. Taught me. He was the best father anyone could ever have.

"There isn't a day that goes by where I don't think about you Dad. We all miss you!"

And Martin Coughlan wasn't the only Irish man working on a construction job at the World Trade Center on the day that Muslim fanatics rocked the Big Apple.

Sligo man Kieran Gorman (34) lived in the Bronx neighbourhood of New York with his wife Anne and two sons. The Carrowcurragh native, a cousin of RTE's northern correspondent Tommy Gorman, was a former goalkeeper with Sligo and is remembered by his friends as a "big strong handsome fellow". He had been based in the US for nine years.

On the eve of the attacks, he returned from a holiday to Ireland with his pregnant wife to find a message on his answering-machine asking if he could start work early on a construction job at the World Trade Center. Kieran wasn't supposed to return to work for a few days more, but he decided to take the work, mindful of the new addition that would soon be joining their brood. Tragically, the devoted family man would live to regret his decision.

Like Martin Coughlan, the Sligo man phoned his wife on the morning of 9/11 to reassure her that, while there had been an explosion, he was unhurt and was making his way to ground level from the 97th floor of the South Tower.

In the days that followed, his wife Anne, who grew up near Omagh in Co Tyrone, waited by the phone for news of her husband. Kieran's widowed mother Ann, who lived in Lavagh, and his sister and brothers in Ireland also prayed that he would be found alive.

Sadly, the call that he had been found alive never came — and the loving father never made it home to see the birth of his third son, Kieran Jnr, who was born a few weeks later.

Six months after the attack, his body was found at Ground Zero and flown home for a funeral at Mullinabreena Church.

Speaking at the funeral, family friend and local priest Fr Tom Johnston praised the "painstaking perseverance" of rescue workers who recovered victims. Anne Gorman and her three sons, Barry, Gavin and Kieran Jnr, have since moved from the couple's Bronx home back to Sligo to be close to family members — their American dream over.

Bubbly blonde Dubliner Joanne Cregan (32) was one of so many Irish who moved across the Atlantic to live the "high life" in New York. As an employee of New York financial firm Cantor Fitzgerald, she had moved over with her sister and best friend Grace in the late 90s and instantly fell in love with the city that never sleeps.

The sisters bought identical apartments just two floors apart in the same Brooklyn Heights building, sent each other email messages throughout the day and watched television together every night. "She was an excellent big sister," Grace said. "Sometimes it just hits me that I'll never see her again. I won't get to grow old with her."

Tragically Joanne, who loved kids, was about to become the godmother of three babies — but she never lived to see her godchildren. The Churchtown native was on the 105th floor of the North Tower in the E Speed division of her company when the first plane struck.

Stranded high in the tower, a few floors above the impact zone of the hijacked plane, her escape route was treacherous and ultimately impossible. Cantor Fitzgerald lost 658 employees — all of the employees in the office at the time of the attacks. This equated to about two-thirds of its workforce, considerably more than any other of the World Trade Center tenants or New York City Police Department and New York City Fire Department.

Amazingly, as the 10-year anniversary of the attacks approach, Joanne's mother Mary has spoken about how she has found the strength to forgive those who took her daughter's life away. "We all feel blessed that we hold no hatred," she said. "Why perpetuate the poison? Why continue the hatred?"

Drimnagh native Patrick Currivan (52) was on the first plane to hit the North Tower of the World Trade Center. Like many others who lost loved ones on that fateful September day, Patrick's sister, Helen Currivan Redden, recalled waking that morning with deep a sense unease. "I don't feel right," she remembers telling her husband Martin.

Helen was the youngest of three children and the only girl in the Currivan family. Her other brother, Dan, a marine engineer, was on a ship that was sailing from Venezuela to Boston. As it happened, he, too, later said that he felt bad that morning. "It must be something in the genes," Helen said.

Just before 8am, at 1pm Irish time, American Airlines Flight 11 took off from Logan Airport in Boston heading for Los Angeles. There were 81 passengers on board and Patrick Currivan was seated in row 10. There had been a dinner party the night before and his sister said that she likes to think that maybe her brother had taken the opportunity to sleep — that maybe he wasn't awake when his world spun out of control.

Flight attendants were preparing for cabin service when the hijackers struck. Two flight attendants were stabbed and a first-class passenger, Daniel Lewin, had his throat slashed. It is believed that the chief hijacker, Egyptian Mohammed Atta, took over the controls in the cockpit, because he was the only one with flight training. But almost half an hour into the crisis most of the passengers, probably including Patrick, still believed it was a medical emergency.

At 8.46pm, the plane flew straight into the North Tower of the World Trade Center.

Helen's husband came to tell her that something bad was happening in America. The couple knew Patrick was in Boston but did not know he was caught up in the disaster. Even so, Martin was sufficiently concerned to ring Patrick's mobile phone at about 3.30pm Irish time and leave a message to call him back.

Patrick had flown from Paris to Boston a few days before. He had a high-powered job in computers and stockbroking in the French capital as vice president at Atos-Euronext, but had previously worked in Boston and still had a house there, as well as many friends. He had stopped off to see them before heading onwards to LA for a conference.

At about 8.45pm on the evening of September 11, seven hours after the tragedy, Martin took a phone call from David Smith, Patrick's lawyer and best friend. It had been that confirmed Patrick had been on the plane. His survival was out of the question.

Helen's anger towards the hijackers who stole her brother's life is still great. "They murdered him and all those other people."

Helen had no body to bury and was told that, in order to buy a plot in the graveyard and put up a memorial, you had to have a body. In the end she had a plaque made in his honour and this was set into the cemetery wall. The late US senator Edward Kennedy sent her an American flag which was flown over the US Capitol in Washington DC in memory of the 9/11 victims. It is now on display in a glass case at her home in Rush in north Co Dublin.

Helen said she has drawn on her brother's zest for life to help her through the grief of his untimely passing. "My brother would be horrified if he thought there was weeping and gnashing of teeth," she said. "He would not like to be mourned in that sense. He had too much of a thirst for life."

Friends of the Trinity graduate remember an adventurous man who loved to travel. "Whatever chance he got he quizzed people," said Kathy Marshall, a neighbor who visited Egypt with him. "He really delved into their understanding and knowledge of their own country, where they were and who they were, and he constantly asked questions. And if you were smart, you stood around and waited to hear the answers."

Kathy's husband Paul recalled that Patrick had traveled extensively on the Silk Road and in Syria, and was particularly interested in the richness of Islamic culture, visiting mosque after mosque in Cairo.

Slain Abroad

September 11, 2001 may well go down as the bloodiest day in the history of the Irish people. In fact, the first recorded casualty of the attacks was Father Mychal Judge, the beloved Irish American priest who was a beacon in New York's Irish community. The son of immigrants from Co Leitrim, Fr Judge was chaplain of the Fire Department of New York.

Upon hearing the news that the World Trade Center had been hit, Fr Judge rushed to the site. He was met by the Mayor of New York, Rudolph Giuliani, who asked him to pray for the city and its victims. Judge administered last rites to some lying on the streets, then entered the lobby of the World Trade Center North Tower, where an emergency command post was organized. There he continued offering aid and prayers for the rescuers, the injured and dead.

When the South Tower collapsed at 9.59am, debris went flying through the North Tower lobby, killing many inside, including Fr Judge. At the moment he was struck in the head and killed, Fr Judge was repeatedly praying aloud: "Jesus, please end this right now! God please end this!", according his biographer and *New York Daily News* columnist Michael Daly.

In all, 2,996 people lost their lives in the terrorist attacks. Of these, six were born in Ireland — but many more killed in the atrocity were of Irish descent. Based on family names and individual stories, there were many hundreds of American dead with Irish heritage, including Americans who through parents or grandparents had become Irish citizens. It is now estimated that 1,000 people who were of Irish descent or of Irish birth were lost in the violent events on that day.

The true number of the dead may never be known because there are so many Irish people working illegally in New York. Yet the heroics of firefighters, police officers and emergency workers of Irish descent will forever be remembered alongside office workers and plane passengers who displayed immense courage. Many who died were leaders in their chosen professions. In honour of this the Irish government was one of the first administrations in the world to announce a national day of mourning.

The death towers

It is no exaggeration to state that the bloody events of that day changed the world forever. It was the day when al Qaeda and its Saudi millionaire leader Osama bin Laden became the world's most notorious murderers. It led to wars in Afghanistan and Iraq. To this day, the images of the carnage have been seared onto our minds.

For almost a decade, bin Laden remained at the top of the US Most Wanted list despite a $25m (€17m) bounty on his head. Hunted by special forces in Afghanistan and Pakistan, he continued to orchestrate terrorist attacks, murdering innocent civilians in Bali, Madrid, London and Istanbul.

Former US President George W Bush tried and failed to track him down. Meanwhile, al-Qaeda continued to release time-sensitive and professionally-verified videos demonstrating bin Laden's survival.

Then, on May 1, 2011, US President Barack Obama announced to the world that the architect of the 9/11 attacks, the man who gave the attacks the green light, had been killed by US forces in Pakistan.

Bin Laden was shot dead at a compound near Islamabad in a ground operation based on US intelligence. Three other men — one of bin Laden's sons and two couriers — were killed in the raid. Americans reacted to the news with joy, filling the streets of New York. Crowds gathered outside the White House in Washington DC, chanting "USA, USA" after the news broke.

The bogeyman of the West, who for so long had evaded capture, was shot twice, once in the chest and once in the head. His body was later buried at sea. It was a major victory for the US and in particular Barack Obama, who described it as "the most significant achievement to date in our nation's effort to defeat al-Qaeda".

Irish relatives of the 9/11 attacks reacted positively to the news. Ruth McCourt's brother Ronnie said he felt vindicated. "The world has gotten rid of a Hitler," he said. "That is how important this man's death is. He was evil and had to be made pay for the lives of nearly 3,000 people that he had murdered.

It is a great day for the US and the wider world to know that he is now gone."

It was also an emotional time for Martin Coughlan's family. While happy to hear that the terrorist leader had been killed, Martin's widow Catherine and daughter Denise felt it might not be the end to the bloodshed. "It is good that he is no longer able to carry out attacks but I wonder how long it will be before his group try to get revenge?"

With bin Laden now dead, the focus of the bereaved has shifted to getting justice in relation to the other five 9/11 suspects, including mastermind Khalid Sheikh Mohammed, who are currently being held at the Guantanamo Bay detention facility in Cuba. Since his capture in Pakistan in 2003, Khalid Sheikh Mohammed has confessed to planning the 9/11 attacks, the attack on the USS Cole, and other terrorism activities including the beheading of *Wall Street Journal* reporter Daniel Pearl. Plans to hold his trial and those of four other notorious terrorism suspects in New York were scrapped in 2010 when projected security rocketed. President Obama says he is now reconsidering the idea of military trials at Guantanamo Bay.

For men like Ronnie Clifford, who lost his sister and his niece, real closure cannot come until he sees those responsible locked up. "My family, the Cliffords of Cork, along with the rest of the 9/11 victims are still waiting for President Barack Obama to make good on his promise to bring the 9/11 terrorists to trial," Ronnie said.

"President Obama met with the victims' families two years ago in Washington, D.C., and promised 'swift and certain justice' for the terrorists. Since then, however, nothing effectual or determinative has been accomplished in order to move forward with a trial. It's now almost 10 years since the 9/11 violent carnage of innocent victims, and still there are no scheduled proceedings to bring the terrorists to trial. We have gotten rid of bin Laden — now we must see proper justice dispensed for this collective heinous crime."

AMY FITZPATRICK:
Abducted?

HER ANGELIC face filled the entire screen.

As the highly-paid footballers filed off the pitch at La Rosaleda Stadium, the massive photograph of the young teenager must surely have caught the eye of some of the 30,000 fans sitting in their stands. The spectators had just watched the first half of a pulsating soccer match between Malaga and visitors Real Madrid in Spain's premier division, La Liga.

After 10 minutes of play, underdogs Malaga took a shock lead with a well-worked goal from Felipe Caicedo. Madrid, whose team included stars such as Cristiano Ronaldo, Xabi Alonso, Rafael Van Der Vaart and Iker Casillas, launched attack after attack for the remaining 35 minutes of the half — but could not break down a resolute Malaga defence.

Most of the spectators crammed into the stadium on the outskirts of Malaga probably didn't even take a second glance at the photograph of the pale, innocent looking teenager with the wide eyes as it flashed up on the huge scoreboard dominating one end of the stadium. The bulk of the crowd would have been too busy talking about the goal, or scurrying to the bar to get a quick beer before the second half began.

But some of them will have looked up. And some of them

will have, even briefly, wondered why her photograph was being displayed so prominently during the match interval.

They got their answer a few seconds later. For, as well as the girl's image, her identity was also flashed up on the screen.

Her name was Amy Fitzpatrick. The crowd were also told, in English and Spanish, that Amy was 15 when she disappeared on January 1, 2008, as she walked home in Riviera del Sol, a sun resort 40 miles south of Malaga.

They were also told that there had been no sighting of her since; that her mother wanted her back and that anyone with even the smallest piece of information could contact a special hotline. The image was only up on the screen for a few minutes, but for Amy's driven mother Audrey, it was a great success. Even though, as expected, no-one came forward with the nugget of information she had been craving that would solve the mystery of her daughter's disappearance, it was still a good day's work for the Dublin-born mother-of-two.

The fact that 30,000 were shown Amy's picture, showed Audrey that her daughter was not forgotten about.

It showed her that Amy counted, not only to herself, but to the people who let her display the photograph on the scoreboard — and to the fans who had bothered to look up, even briefly. It showed that, with a little bit of imagination and lots of hard work, there were still plenty of ways of keeping Amy in the public eye — even though she had not been seen for almost 30 months.

And, most important of all, Sunday, May 16, 2010 — the day of the game and the day of the half-time appeal — showed one overriding truth: Audrey would never, ever, give up on her little girl.

She didn't look back as she walked along the alleyway.

It was just after 9pm on New Year's Day, 2008, and a young Irish girl was making her way home in the Costa del Sol after spending the previous night with the family of her best friend.

Amy Fitzpatrick, who was just 15, said goodbye to her pal, Ashley Rose, on the steps of her home at around 10pm.

Amy had spent New Year's Eve babysitting with Ashley, who was slightly younger than her, at 13.

On New Year's night, she told Ashley she wanted to stay, but Ashley's mum, hairdressing salon owner Debbie, said it would be better if she went home to her own mum.

Amy asked for a lift. But Debbie, who had driven her home dozens of times without a problem, said she couldn't — she had gone out the previous night to usher in 2008 in style and had left her car at the bar where she had been celebrating.

Amy then said she would walk home.

From Ashley's house, in Calle Los Olivos, it was a walk of less than a mile to Amy's home in the Las Lomas de Riviera complex — a route she had taken dozens of times in the past year or so. It would only have taken her around 20 minutes to get back to her house.

She went out the front door, turned left at the gate and walked up the road around 100 yards. From there, her route home was a simple one — take the next left which brought her up a street with a steep incline around 200 metres long.

At the end of that street, there was a little alleyway which would have brought her out on to an open piece of ground.

This track, over a small hill, was a shortcut used by local people every day to get to the Riviera del Sol resort from Amy's family home in the Las Lomas complex.

It was dark at that time of the evening, and Amy often confided in Ashley that she did not like taking that route home. "She used to use that walk all the time although I told her it was not safe. My mum would not let me walk through there at night," Ashley said. "It is dark and scary and I know a few weeks prior that Amy got a fright when she heard a woman screaming in one of the homes nearby. That was followed by a smashing sound. She told me she was really scared and that she ran all the way home."

But, despite her fears, she continued using the shortcut, because it took so much time off her journey home.

Once she was finished with the track, she would have gotten back onto a well-lit street and her complex was at the top of the hill, around half a mile away. All in, she would have been home, safe, within 20 minutes.

The two houses were in the Riviera del Sol holiday resort, which is part of the greater Calahonda complex. That, in turn, is around 10 miles south of Fuengirola, one of the best known holiday sun spots on the Costa del Sol in south east Spain.

Fuengirola and Calahonda welcome tens of thousands of tourists, particularly from Ireland and Britain, every year.

They come for the almost guaranteed sun and temperatures quite often breach the 30°C mark — especially in July and August.

But plenty of Irish and British people have gone one step further than going to Fuengirola for a fortnight's sun holiday in the summer — hundreds of them have fallen for the undoubted lure of the area and have set up home there.

Amy's mother, Audrey, was one such person who fell for the area. With Amy, her son Dean and her partner Dave Mahon, she moved from her native north Dublin to settle in Riviera del Sol in 2004. She and Dave, also from Dublin, set up their own rental agency, which was busy and successful.

As she left Ashley's home, 15-year-old Amy was not a happy girl. She could not settle in Spain and was desperate to go back to Dublin, where her father Christopher still lived.

She had been planning to go back for a holiday on St Stephen's Day, but that trip was cancelled at the last moment. She had, however, been told that another trip would be organised in the coming weeks.

According to Ashley, that trip could not come quickly enough. She didn't like Spain and had gotten a rough time from other teenagers. "She really didn't like Spain at all," Ashley admitted. "She kept on saying how much she hated the place and wanted to go back home to Ireland. I think it was because of all the bullying. She had a terrible time. A lot of people bullied her, both mentally and physically — it was terrible. She went to a local school and she got bullied there and then she went to an international school and got bullied there as well.

"A lot of people didn't like her, but that's because they didn't know her. She had a reputation as being a bit strange, but that was unfair. If people took the time to get to know her they would have realised she was just the same as everyone else."

Amy left Ashley's house at around 10pm. "She was in great form. We were laughing and joking and she told me how lucky she was to have a friend like me," Ashley recalled.

Ashley offered to walk part of the way with her, but Amy declined. She told her best friend she would be back to see her at 6pm the following day.

But at 1pm, five hours before Amy was due back, Ashley's mum Debbie got a phone call that made her world stop turning.

The person on the other line was Audrey, Amy's mum. She was asking how her daughter was getting on. Debbie, with her heart in her mouth, told Audrey that Amy had left her house the previous night to walk home.

"I really regret not telling her she could stay now," Debbie would say later. "I just told her I thought she should go home to her mother. The girls were here for some time and then they went on the bus to Fuengirola. I phoned Ashley and told her to get back home straight away.

"When they arrived back they had dinner here that evening. They went out for a short time and then when they returned Amy collected her clothes which she carried in a red and white Berska bag. When something like this happens it makes you aware and this is a wake-up call for all us parents.

"You always think your children are going to be OK and hopefully Amy will be back safe to us. But it is very worrying as she always contacted Ashley no matter what and she would never leave it so long without being in touch with her."

The two women's phone conversation plunged Audrey into a living nightmare that continues to this day.

By the time the phone call was made, Amy had been missing for 15 hours — and nobody had had a clue she was gone.

Immediately, frantically, Audrey and her partner Dave began ringing around Amy's other friends to see if she had gone to them after leaving Ashley's house.

The 15-year-old who was so unhappy had run away from home several times before, but had always been in contact and kept in touch. And, because she was not in her own country, there were only a few places that she could go to. There were, for example, no relations living anywhere near where she could go. The only realistic option was that she had gone to a friend's house instead of going home.

But there was only one problem — none of her other friends had heard from her either. Audrey knew what she had to do. She picked up the phone and called the police. Her girl was missing.

Cops on the Costa del Sol deal with hundreds of missing persons' cases every year, with most disappearances being resolved quickly. The missing person usually disappears for only a few hours or days, before coming back home — or getting in touch with their family to say they are OK.

But Amy was different. There was no communication from her at all and, within minutes, her mother was becoming increasingly worried. Spanish cops began an immediate search for her, combing the route she would have taken for even the slightest clue. But there was nothing: no clothes, no forensic evidence, no sightings, and no sign of a struggle — no CCTV of her. Nothing. She had, quite simply, vanished.

The family initially believed it was possible — but unlikely — that she may have decided to run away to Ireland.

Her father Christopher still lives in Dublin and she grew up in the Coolock area of the city. But she had no money, no mobile phone and no passport — which meant she had no way of getting back home.

As the hours and days passed, Audrey and the other members of her family were coming to a frightening conclusion — she had been taken. For them it was unquestionable that she would have run away from home — they knew someone had snatched her. As the cops continued the search for her, Audrey went public in a desperate bid to get her daughter back.

On the Saturday after Amy disappeared, Audrey and Dave — looking pale, drawn and exhausted — held a press conference in a hotel overlooking the sea at Calahonda.

It was, by now, four days since Amy vanished and Audrey was becoming increasingly worried.

News of Amy's disappearance, and the search for her broke on the Friday morning and by Saturday several Irish and British newspapers were in Riviera del Sol, working on the story. Audrey, who had never spoken in front of a camera, realised almost instinctively that she had to speak to the press.

The possibility of putting Amy's image into the public domain was simply too good to ignore.

With Dave at her side, Audrey sat down at a small table and poured her heart out about her missing daughter — and her darkest fears. "I'm beside myself with worry. All I want is for Amy to pick up a phone and ring me or a friend and say she's OK," Audrey said. "At the back of my mind is that horrible fear that something's happened to her.

"The longer this goes on, the worse this gets. I've racked my brains for a reason as to why Amy might want to go off on her own and I can't think of one. She's never done anything like this before. Teenagers are teenagers and we have the odd row. She's spent the night at friends before after we've argued but she's always rung that night or in the morning to say she was OK."

Ashley, Amy's best friend, was just as pessimistic as

Audrey. She believed there was no chance she had run away.

"Amy would never go a day without contacting me. She used to call every evening at 6pm to meet up," she said. "Something bad has had to have happened to her for her not to have contacted me for so many days. I don't believe she has run away although she was unhappy about certain things. I believe she has been abducted and is being held somewhere."

And Ashley had good reason to believe Amy may have been abducted. She told *The Star* just a few days after the disappearance that Amy had confided to her that she had suffered four separate attempts by a man to lure her into a car in the run up to January.

"She told me four times in the weeks before she disappeared of times when a man tried to get her into his car," she said.

"She just said she left my house and was walking up the hill when a man approached and asked if she wanted to get into his car. She told me she said no and walked quickly away. She is streetwise — she's not the sort of girl who would get into a stranger's car anyway."

And, crucially, each of the incidents happened as she walked from Ashley's house to her own — the same route she took on the night she disappeared.

There were also other reasons for the strong fear to exist that Amy had been abducted, and had not run away.

In the weeks prior to Amy's disappearance, several locals spotted a man in a white car trying to pick up children and take them away. That was in the same general area where Amy vanished.

One local said: "We don't know if the two are connected but everyone is very concerned. People had spoken about it and were keeping a close eye on their kids. He was supposed to be stopping kids and trying to get them to go off with him."

And it would not be the first time that sexual predators had been operating in the same area.

The towns around Riviera del Sol were the hunting ground of Costa killer Tony King. He is currently serving 62 years in jail in Spain after being convicted of the murders of

Abducted?

Spanish teenagers Rocio Wanninkhof and Sonia Carabantes and a separate attempted rape.

Wanninkhof (19) was stabbed to death in October 1999 in Mijas Costa near Fuengirola as she walked home to get ready for a night out with her boyfriend. She worked as an au pair to British businessman Cliff Stanford, founder of technology company Redbus Interhouse, at his summer home on the Costa del Sol. Sonia Carabantes (17) was beaten semi-conscious, kidnapped and strangled to death before being dumped partially naked on waste ground in mountains behind the coast in August 2003.

King, now 45, served time in a UK jail for a series of attacks on women in north London before changing his birth surname of Bromwich by deed poll and emigrating. And, because Calahonda and Riviera del Sol had a significant transient population, it would be easy for any predator to hide there. There were so many resorts and estates, called urbanisaciones in Spanish, that cops could not keep an eye on everyone.

Cops searching for Amy had a twin track approach to the investigation. On the one hand, they expected — hoped, even — that she had run away.

Countless teenagers do that in every country every year. Most of them return home within a few days, a fortnight at most. But, as every day passed and nothing was heard from her, the police in her case began to suspect more and more that, as her family and friends feared, she had been abducted.

While some officers searched the area around Calle Los Olivos and the path she should have taken home, others called on a host of young people who knew Amy to see if they had seen her in recent days.

One of the first to be visited was Amy's ex boyfriend, English-born Will Short, who was 15 at the time of her disappearance. He said two detectives searched the house he shares outside Riviera del Sol with his mother Lisa and brother Jamal. He said: "These two detectives came in and just looked around the place to see if there was any sign of her. They were checking to see if she was here."

He and Amy had broken up in November, two months before she vanished. "She is a very nice girl, very quiet and like everyone I am worried about her," he said. "I would just say to her 'come home'. Everybody is very upset and everyone is very worried about her."

Unlike Ireland, which in the Garda Siochana has a so-called unitary police force, Spain has several law enforcement agencies. And three separate police units were involved in the hunt for Amy from the start. The first was the Policia Local, or local police. They are controlled by the local town hall.

They deal with largely minor matters, such as traffic control and public order. But they are armed and mount numerous patrols in the Calahonda area — often having to arrest drunken tourists. The next unit is the National Police, or CNP.

The force is responsible for security in urban areas and also has responsibility for national security, terrorism, national criminal investigations, judicial matters and immigration.

It is responsible for border control and drug offences. The National Police operates in all the capitals of Spain's provinces and other large towns.

The third unit, however, is the most famous to foreigners and was the lead investigation unit in the Amy case. The Civil Guard, or Guardia Civil, are famous for their olive green uniforms and no-nonsense manner. They are technically part of the armed forces and were formed in 1844.

They are tasked with ensuring public safety and were originally charged with policing rural areas of Spain — which include Calahonda. But their role has now been extended to include anti-terrorism, traffic policing on main roads and the protection of ports and airports.

Because Amy disappeared in an area that was largely rural and outside the main urban sprawls in southern Spain, it was the Guardia Civil who were the main investigators in the case. The officer in charge of the investigation was Teniente Jose Bordero.

That rank translates as 1st Lieutenant and is roughly the equivalent of a superintendent in the Garda Siochana.

Abducted?

His office was based in Fuengirola and that was the centre of the probe into Amy's disappearance from day one.

It was his decision, a week after Amy was reported missing, to launch the first major move in the case.

It was time for a large-scale search.

It was dawn on Wednesday, January 9, 2008. As the sun rose over Riviera Del Sol, there was still no sign of Amy. Nothing stirred in the resort town, most of the holidaymakers enjoying some New Year's sun were still in their beds, sleeping off the excesses of the night before. But, just four miles away, the village of Mijas Costa was a hive activity. On a municipal football pitch, the noise was almost deafening.

Some 200 members of Guardia Civil, the Policia Local and Policia Nacional were congregating on the pitch, and were joined by firefighters, civil protection officers and even volunteers from the Red Cross. They were all united in one common purpose — taking part in a massive search for Amy.

And it wasn't just humans who were involved – specialist dogs were flown in from Madrid. These so-called cadaver dogs were trained to find bodies. Dead bodies. Helicopters and a host of different off-road vehicles were also to be used.

The Guardia Civil had also discussed the idea of using civilian volunteers in the search, but top brass later rowed back on that option — much to the annoyance of several Irish ex-pats who wanted to help. However a handful of people did still show up at the site. One of them, Catherine Higgins, said she just wanted to help. Ms Higgins, who runs the Spanish Arch pub in Fuengirola, said: "The Irish community is very concerned. People just want to help."

The search began at 8am, when it was fully daylight, and was marshalled with the military precision one would expect from the Guardia Civil. The officers split up into eight groups and mounted a relentless search of the area around where Amy was last seen — stretching 6km each way. The officers scoured undergrowth, hills, bushes, gorges, ravines and property for any sign of Amy — but found nothing.

There was a major drama an hour into the search when a specialist search team found leggings in a deep ravine, around 150 metres from the shortcut that Amy would have taken on her way home the night she disappeared. Although she was wearing brown velour track-suit bottoms when she vanished, she was carrying a pair of black leggings in her bag at the time. But, after an examination, Spanish detectives said they were satisfied the leggings were not the pair owned by Amy.

The leggings were the only items of interest found that day and, as darkness fell, the Spanish police called off the search, but vowed it would continue.

Shortly after the leggings were found, Amy's father Christopher arrived at the scene. He had been frantically trying to get the 1,500 miles from Dublin to the Costa del Sol as soon as he heard that Amy was in trouble. He arrived just as the search was ongoing.

The first thing he learned was that the leggings were found. His heart was in his mouth until he was told they were not Amy's. "That's great news — thank God," he sighed. But, as he stood on the path that his daughter took on the night she disappeared, Christopher could not help being pessimistic.

His heart was telling him that there was a still a chance Amy would come back and say she had just gone away for a few days, but his head was telling him otherwise. "The longer this goes on, the less likely it looks that she will come back alive," he admitted. "I wanted to be here for the search in case they find something. I'm now only a stone's throw away from the search site rather than in a different country. So I will be able to get to anywhere here quickly if anything is found."

But nothing was found. Audrey and Christopher were united in their grief. But there was another reason why Christopher, who was ill at the time, had braved the journey to Spain — he wanted to quash the rumours circulating that Amy had left Calahonda and travelled back to his home in Dublin.

Abducted?

Christopher's sister, Christine Kenny, said the rumours were devastating him. "These rumours are just ridiculous," she insisted. "They are saying that Chris has Amy back at his house all the time — it's scandalous. What would he be doing over here if she was back in Ireland? She doesn't even have a passport — how could she have gotten to Ireland in the first place? This was one of the reasons why we came to Spain — to show people Amy wasn't with Chris."

While there were plenty of rumours that Amy had run away, they were just that — rumours. Nobody had any idea what had happened to her. But, two weeks after her disappearance Spanish cops started briefing local media that they were beginning to believe that she had, after all, run away.

Several respected Spanish newspapers carried bizarre claims from police sources that Amy and her friends may have conspired to get her out of the country — and back to Ireland. One local newspaper, *La Opinion De Malaga*, exclaimed: "The theory of a pact of silence is based on the possibility that Amy may have received the help of someone she knew to get her to Gibraltar (around 60 miles from Fuengirola). That would have been by the local motorway or the port of Cabopino, some five miles from Amy's home, in a pleasure boat. Once in Gibraltar airport, she could easily have gotten through passport control if she was accompanied by an adult."

But there was only one problem — Amy did not have a passport. How could she possibly get onto a flight from Gibraltar to the UK and then pass through notoriously tough security at a British airport, before flying on to Ireland?

It just didn't make sense and gave rise to the belief that the Spanish were trying to spin their way out of a problem.

They had no idea where she was, or what happened to her. Perhaps it would be better all round if people began to believe she had gone away of her own free will.

Gardai were called in to carry out investigations back in Ireland, but officers were immediately sceptical that she had somehow managed to make it to Dublin.

One source told *The Star* at the time: "She may well have

done a runner, but it seems highly unlikely she would have made it back to Ireland. She has no passport and that makes it almost impossible for her to get in or out of the country without being noticed. There are no direct flights between Gibraltar and Ireland, so she would have had to have flown in to some UK airport and then on to Dublin, and it is impossible for her to have slipped through two nets."

The implication of the Spanish cops' briefing was clear — they wanted the whole thorny problem of Amy Fitzpatrick and what may have happened to her to just go away.

Within days of the massive search, the Spanish probe began to wind down. By the middle of 2008, only a few months after her disappearance, just five officers were on the case. Amy was officially forgotten.

The authorities may have forgotten about her, but Amy's family simply refused to give up. Driven by the hunger and energy that only loved ones can summon, all her relations — in two countries — began a sustained campaign to keep Amy in the public eye.

Just three weeks after her disappearance, Audrey and Dave held a ceremony in Calahonda on what would be Amy's 16th birthday — February 7. Neither Audrey nor her partner Dave could summon up the strength to attend the party, they were so devastated at all the events of the previous month.

But around 40 of Amy's friends gathered at a venue in Calahonda to celebrate the day — and to remember her.

Amy's brother Dean fought back tears at the party as he made an emotional appeal for her to come back. "Amy, I love you — please come home," Dean, then 17, wrote on one of 16 balloons released to remember Amy on her big day.

It was a bittersweet day for everyone who was there. Ashley Rubio Rose, her best friend and the last person to see Amy before she disappeared, said simply: "It was important to come to the party, we all are thinking of her."

But days turned into weeks, weeks turned into months and months even turned into years and still there was no trace of Amy. The only constant was that, in Ireland and in Spain, Amy's parents and relatives refused to give up on finding her.

In June 2008, Audrey flew back into Dublin and visited St Brendan's in Coolock village, the church where Amy was baptised, made her first Communion and Confirmation. A special Mass was even held at the church to remember her.

For Audrey, there were mixed emotions as she walked into the church. "Being back in the church is a great comfort to us because it holds so many of our lovely memories of every stage of Amy's life," she said. "It's all the sadder because she's not with us, but we are still praying everyday that she gets in touch."

A few months later, in August, Amy's granny Maura Donohoe (80) begged Irish holidaymakers heading to the Calahonda area to be on the lookout for her precious granddaughter. And she spoke candidly of her fears that Amy might not be found for a long time.

"I'm starting to worry the search for her might turn into years. I've noticed families of some missing people have been waiting for years," said Maura. "As the months go by, it gets more tiring. The longer it goes on, the worse it's been getting. We've always been lighting candles for Amy in the church and my eyes still fill with tears when people ask me about her.

"I'll always remember the conversation I had with Amy on the telephone on the day before she disappeared. She had been looking forward to a trip home to Ireland and she was so delighted. These days, I find myself talking to her photograph."

Shortly after that, the Spanish dropped the pretence that she had probably run away and admitted that it was more likely Amy had been abducted. A leading local government official in Andalusia, the region of southern Spain that includes Calahonda, admitted that it was less likely she had left the area voluntarily. Juan Jose Lopez Garzon admitted: "As each day goes by, the theory that she left of her own free will loses strength.

"We haven't completely ruled it out, but if that was the case we would have expected someone to have seen her or spoken to her by now." But he insisted: "The investigation is not being scaled down and it will not happen."

Some members of Amy's family found it hard to agree with that claim. Her aunt, Christine, who even hired her own private investigator to probe Amy's disappearance, was deeply critical of the Spanish cops and their attitude to the case by July 2009 — 18 months after she had gone missing.

Christine believed the Spanish had, effectively, shelved the case. "Every time we contact the consulate in Spain they tell us there are no updates," Christine said. "If the case was still being pursued, surely they would be able to say people are still being questioned but that isn't happening. It's been 18 months now and there is still no sign of a 17-year-old Irish citizen."

Despite all the setbacks, Audrey steadfastly kept up her campaign to keep her daughter in the public eye — something she does to this day. She is always available to talk to any journalist who shows an interest in the case and she and Dave Mahon have spent a fortune travelling around Europe trying to rally interest in Amy. They have even gone as far as Morocco, amid fears that Amy may have been abducted and transported to the north African country. She has gone to several tourist hotspots in Spain, even to the Canary Islands off the African coast, handing out flyers and posters of her daughter.

And there has not just been an emotional toll — her finances have taken a hammering from the money she has spent on her relentless, unending campaign. In mid 2009, things got so bad that she was warned she may lose her home because she had been unable to pay the mortgage for several months. She and Dave had spent more than €200,000 hunting for Amy, and were simply unable to pay their €2,000-a-month mortgage.

"Financially it's getting harder," she admitted. "We were lucky enough at the start that we weren't poor. We had savings, but obviously we've used up all that. You can't keep it going unless you have money. So Dave is trying his best now to get back into work as well, which is not very easy to do because of the way real estate is. I would say we've spent a couple of hundred grand, when you think of flights and accommodation and posters.

"Without working, everything went down to zero. There is a way of checking on your phone how much credit you have used — Dave found it on his phone and he has used €10,000 in the last year. That's just his phone, not including mine."

She also spoke of how she was desperate to stay in the family home because she believed Amy could walk back in at any second. But now, more than three years after her disappearance, Audrey is still waiting, still hoping.

The leads in the case dried up very quickly. Within days it became clear that Amy Fitzpatrick, a vibrant young girl with everything to live for, had simply vanished off the face of the earth. There were no sightings, no phone calls, no emails, no Bebo messages. Nothing.

While the family clung desperately to the hope that she would turn up, Spanish police sources were more fatalistic.

Law enforcement sources in Spain told *The Star* late last year, almost three years after she was last seen, that they had no hope Amy was alive.

One officer said: "With three years gone now, the likelihood is that she was murdered that night. It is very rare for a girl of that age to disappear and for nobody to hear from her since. That must lead to the conclusion that she is dead."

They say the most likely scenario is she was abducted as she walked home, before being murdered and secretly buried.

But if she was abducted and killed that January night, who was responsible?

Police officers all over the world work on percentages. When faced with a mystery, they tend to go back to basics and examine the most likely scenario — they tend not to do conspiracy theories. They know, for example, that if a woman is beaten to death in her own home, the likelihood is that it was her husband or spouse. Some 80 per cent of females killed in such circumstances are murdered by someone they knew.

They also know it is likely that, in the case of Amy, the attacker would have known her. Although the case of Tony King in the Costa del Sol does show there are strange killers about, most children who are murdered are killed by someone they know. One theory is that Amy was approached by a man she knew, who lured her into his vehicle and drove off.

That is certainly one theory Audrey and Dave followed. They say Spanish authorities had done nothing to track down a "suspicious" Englishman who disappeared from his Costa del Sol home after Amy went missing.

Audrey said last year: "Almost a year and a half ago we gave the Guardia Civil the name of a well-known criminal. We also gave this to the Irish government and the Irish Embassy here in Spain and, as far as we know, nothing has been done about it. This person left Spain after meeting Dave and denying ever knowing Amy despite the fact he had told other people Amy had been in his house. At the time he met Dave, he joked about sleeping with Amy's 14-year-old friend.

"He's nearly 50 and was carrying a gun. We've acquired the guy's full name, his Spanish address, his English address, his credit card number and the name of the prison in the UK he was in as of last year.

"The Guardia Civil have gone to Spanish courts for permission to ask the English authorities to investigate this man but they've been refused. We don't know whether it's bureaucracy of Spanish politicians trying to push us under the carpet because we're pushing too much."

The author can confirm the man in question is in an English prison. Maybe, just maybe, he holds the answer to the mystery of what happened to Amy.

And maybe one day, Audrey will find out exactly what happened to Amy. But until then, all she can do is hope and pray that one day her cherished little girl will walk back into her home, and back into their lives.

SUGG AND COATES:
Costa crime murders

T HE smell of death was stomach-churning.
It hung heavy and acrid over the small industrial estate on Spain's Costa Blanca, enveloping the three Irish
detectives and their Spanish colleagues in a stench that was
vicious and overpowering.

It got into the police officers' clothes, insinuated its way into
their hair and, of course, assailed their nostrils.

They simply could not get away from it. Even if they walked
several hundred feet away from the crime scene, the smell
chased after them, pummelling their senses.

But coping with the stink was the last thing on their minds.

For the three Garda detectives were now preoccupied with
contacting their superiors in Dublin to break the news to
them.

Standing at the entrance to a warehouse in Catral, 27 miles
south-west of the Spanish sun resort of Alicante, it must have
been almost impossible for the officers from the Garda National Drugs Unit to contain their excitement.

For no more than 50 feet from where they stood lay the
gruesome answer to one of the most enduring mysteries in
modern Irish gangland history.

The skeletal remains of two young, brutal and psychotic

Irish criminals had only moments earlier been excavated from a concrete grave into which their callous killer had dumped them after he had shot each of them in the head at close range with a semi-automatic pistol.

The discovery was made when officers from the Policia Nacional — the Spanish national police force — dug up the foundations of the lock-up in July 2006. And it brought an end to a two-and-a-half year investigation that began with a snippet of information in January 2004.

Gardai in Dublin learned from sources there that Ireland's most infamous criminals of their era, Shane Coates and Stephen Sugg, had disappeared from their apartment in the town of Torrevieja.

From day one, the intelligence suggested that both men — well-known to every garda in Dublin for their sadism and violence — had been murdered by other criminals.

But there was only one problem: there were no bodies. Their disappearance continued to be classified as unsolved until a sunny morning in July 2006.

Gardai had spent thousands of man hours trying to solve the mystery. They had enlisted the help of the Guardia Civil and Policia Nacional in Spain. They had chased down dozens of leads both in Ireland and on the Spanish east coast. The force had, for almost two-and-a-half years, simply refused to give up.

And now, thanks to the dedication and old fashioned agent handling skills of two detectives on the ground in west Dublin, the mystery had finally been solved.

Buried deep in concrete lay the skeletal remains of two of Ireland's most dangerous, most psychotic and most brutal gangsters. Thugs who terrorised men, women and children in their native Blanchardstown, west Dublin for years.

Thugs who burned a grandmother's breast with cigarettes while her young grandson sat watching.

Thugs who sliced an addict's face apart with a carpet knife, just because he owed them a few hundred euro for heroin.

Thugs who shot dead a drug-dealer after he laughed in their

faces when they told him they wanted to take over his patch.

Thugs who, at one stage, ran the biggest drugs gang in Dublin.

And thugs who, after a series of confrontations with gardai and other criminals, fled Ireland to start a new life on the Spanish Costa del Crime.

Shane Coates and Stephen Sugg were the leaders of the infamous Westies drugs and robbery gang that held sway in the Blanchardstown area of Dublin for almost a decade. They thought all their problems would be over when they decamped to Torrevieja in late 2003.

Thousands of Irish people travel to Torrevieja for a fortnight's holiday every year. It's only around two hours by plane from Dublin and Irish holidaymakers are served by more than a dozen flights a week.

The vast majority of Irish people who go there are, of course, decent people who would never even think of breaking the law.

They come for the sun, sangria and whatever else they can get. For many Irish holidaymakers, especially hard-working young men and women from Dublin who want a well-earned two weeks away from the rat race, Torrevieja is holiday central.

But the area around Torrevieja and Alicante also has its dark side. Over the years, several Irish gangsters have moved to the area — eager for not only the sun, but also the way of life it offers.

Like many eastern Spanish sun resorts, the Torrevieja area presents a perfect home from home for Irish gangsters. It has guaranteed sun, but it also has Irish pubs, fast food outlets, nightlife and plenty of other Irish people living there so they will not stand out. It is, in effect, Ireland with guaranteed sunshine.

But it is also a major international crime hub. Gangsters from all the cold European climates seem to like living there. Spanish cops are not only battling with Irish crime bosses living there, but also criminals from Britain and, in the past few years, Russia.

The presence in the area of so many criminals made it an obvious choice for Sugg and Coates when they decided to get out of Ireland in late 2003. Not only did it present them with the chance to lie low for a while, but it also gave the chance to carve out a nice new drugs market.

They knew that if they left Ireland for Torrevieja, they would be out of reach of the Garda detectives who had been relentlessly chipping away at their drugs empire in their native Dublin. But they were also desperately hoping that the rival Dublin crime gang that had been targeting them would forget about them once they left the city.

And, just as importantly, they believed they could set up their own drugs importation business when they settled in Spain.

But, like many other Irish criminals, lifelong pals Sugg and Coates would quickly realise that dreams of making a quick, big buck in Spain were just that: dreams.

And the realisation would come on a hot, Spanish January night as bullets were pumped into the back of both their heads.

The saga of Sugg and Coates ended in Catral, but it began almost 10 years earlier in a rural Irish court.

On Tuesday August 31, 1993, two young men appeared in Navan District Court in Co Meath. They were both charged with breaking into a mini-market in Athlone a few days earlier and stealing items worth £790 – around €1,000 now.

Judge John Brophy remanded one of the men in custody to appear in court the following Friday, although he did set bail

Costa crime murders

at £100.

It was the first time a young Stephen Sugg had appeared in court as an adult: it would not be the last.

Sugg was 18 when he appeared before the formidable Judge Brophy and was, in the eyes of the law, an adult.

But by then, he was already well known to gardai in Dublin's K District — covering Finglas, Blanchardstown and Cabra.

Sugg was born in 1975 and raised in the Corduff area of Blanchardstown — and from an early age, he gave local gardai a headache. Sources have told *The Star* that, from the age of 13 or 14, the young boy was already on the slippery slope of criminality.

"He was involved in joyriding, stealing and public order — anything and everything," one source said. "He just got involved in the wrong crowd as a kid and that was it for him. He picked the wrong path."

By the time he appeared in court in Navan, Sugg was already in the last chance saloon: he had been in several other courts and had been warned by gardai about his behaviour.

But there was nothing that could be done for him — he had already chosen the route of criminality.

One detective who worked in the K District at the time said: "These young fellas were seeing adults in the area involved in drugs and robberies and they could not help but be tempted themselves. You can just imagine seeing someone a few years older than yourself driving around in a flashy BMW, splashing the cash.

"That must be a massive temptation. For many it's either get involved in criminality, or be broke on the dole. There's nothing else for most of these young men in the west and it's no surprise that so many turn to crime."

Shane Coates was another young man who turned to crime as a teenager. He was originally from Corduff, like Sugg, but his family moved to a bungalow in Blanchardstown about seven years after he was born in 1970. The move followed his mother Gina's death from cancer — a tragedy that had a major effect on the young boy.

185

From the age of 11, despite the best efforts of his father Norman, Coates started hanging around with older criminals — particularly those involved in car crime and small-time drug dealing.

By the age of 20, in 1990, he was also well known to gardai. Sources say by this stage Coates was himself dealing in drugs in the Blanchardstown area and becoming increasingly cocky.

"He was very self-confident, even from a young age," one garda recalls. "He had by that stage effectively set up his own crime gang. He was working with a number of young associates, selling drugs in pubs and clubs in the area. He was by no means the biggest dealer in the city, but he had a nice little business going for himself, selling mostly cannabis, heroin and ecstasy."

One of the men working with him was Sugg, who was 18 by late 1993 and had just appeared in front of Judge Brophy in Navan court. Sources say the men were firm friends.

"They had known each other for several years and were really close. Even by this stage, they had a really strong partnership between them. All the young hoods in the area knew that Coates was the boss and Sugg was his right-hand man. Coates was handy with his fists, but so was Sugg. They were frequently involved in rows and beatings against other criminals in the area. They were making a bit of a name for themselves."

Coates, especially, had a reputation for fearsome violence — and that reputation almost cost him his life in August 1994. Eight days earlier, a court would later hear, several female associates of Coates launched a vicious attack on a Blanchardstown woman Alison Dunne. The beating was brutal and sustained and Ms Dunne lost several teeth in the onslaught, as well as having her handbag stolen with her house keys in it.

Her brother Anthony, who was 27 at the time and living at Whitechapel Grove in Dublin 15, spent several days trying to get the handbag and its contents back. On August 12, Dunne was drinking in the Mountainview Inn in Blanchardstown when Shane Coates and others entered. Coates started winding Dunne up about the still missing keys.

A court later heard that Dunne would have had cause to be afraid of Coates, who by then was known for thuggery and violence. Dunne flipped at the taunts from Coates and went home, where he collected his legally-held shotgun. He then went back to the pub brandishing the weapon.

A customer tried to tackle him when he saw the shotgun, and in the ensuing struggle the firearm went off. But that did not stop Dunne. He fired a second shot, hitting his tormentor in the stomach.

Dunne later went to a neighbour and asked him to bring him to the gardai, to whom he made a full and frank statement. Coates somehow survived the shooting, but was forced to wear a colostomy bag for the rest of his life.

Dunne was later charged with shooting Coates, but claimed he had not intended to hit him, merely to frighten him. Dunne was later given a 10-year suspended jail term for the incident.

It was around this time that Sugg, Coates and a few associates who had formed into a loose gang were given a nickname that would last with the pair for the rest of their lives. Shortly after the attempt on his life, locals in Blanchardstown began to call his gang the Westies.

Most people thought the name referred to their power base in Blanchardstown, west Dublin. But, in fact, it was taken from the New York Irish Westies, who ruled the Hell's Kitchen area with extreme violence in the 1970s and 80s. The gang, which never numbered more than 30, was responsible for as many as 600 murders over a 20-year period. Many of their victims met grisly ends, suffering torture and dismemberment.

There could not have been a more apt nickname.

Buoyed by their growing infamy in the area, Coates and Sugg began doling out random beatings to anyone who crossed them. One garda recalls that they targeted vulnerable people and turned them into addicts. "They were really brutal against people who owed them the slightest amount of money, even a few quid," they said. "They would target young teenagers and give them free cannabis or heroin, as a sort of loss leader.

Their rationale was they would give away stuff to kids and then watch them get hooked on gear [heroin] or cannabis. The kids would then become their regular customers."

But when their clients were unable to pay even a small debt, the Irish Westies were almost as vicious as their American counterparts — and showed as little mercy.

On one occasion, a drug addict called Derek 'Smiley' McGuinness was hunted down because he owed the Westies just £480. Sugg sent two of his sidekicks to track him down to Corduff Park in Blanchardstown. One of the men calmly walked up to him, produced an iron bar and smashed it over McGuinness' head.

The blows continued while McGuinness lay defenceless on the ground. Then the other man walked over and kicked him viciously in the head. Attacker number two then pulled out a mobile phone and rang Shane Coates.

"We have Smiley here," he said into the phone. "Do you want to come up to deal with him now?"

Luckily for McGuinness, Coates couldn't get to the park — but unluckily for him, his acolytes were only too happy to launch an even more brutal onslaught on the addict.

"Listen to this," the attacker told Coates and put the phone on the ground. Both men then proceeded to kick, punch and pummel McGuinness on the ground. They didn't stop until every single one of his teeth had been kicked out. Coates could hear the screams on the mobile phone. But there was even worse to come for McGuinness.

Although Coates couldn't make it, Sugg could — and he came armed and dangerous. Sugg appeared while McGuinness was lying seriously wounded on the grass. He could have ordered an end to the beating — but he didn't. Instead, he took out a Stanley knife and started carving up McGuinness' face while his sidekicks held him down. He also cut off a major slice of McGuinness' ear. McGuinness later needed 60 stitches to the horrific injuries to his face.

But then something almost unheard-of happened. Rather than refusing to cooperate with investigating gardai, as often happens, McGuinness decided to make a full statement to detectives.

Normally, victims of such crime refuse to even notify gardai about the assault, such is their fear of being targeted for the worst offence in criminality: talking to the cops. But McGuinness decided he wanted justice and told gardai everything — including the involvement of Sugg and Coates.

Within days Sugg, Coates and two other men were arrested and charged with assault causing harm. Gardai thought they had the breakthrough they were looking for: the Westies by now were seriously in their sight and both leaders were looking at a five-year jail term if they were convicted. The gardai had McGuinness as their star witness: what could go wrong?

Plenty. McGuinness later changed his evidence and said he had lied and exaggerated when he claimed Sugg and Coates were involved. The two other men were jailed, but Sugg and Coates walked free from Dublin Circuit Criminal Court. They must have felt invincible — they had intimidated an attack victim into withdrawing his evidence against them because he was so afraid of them.

The pair probably would have remained low-level drug dealers were it not for the consequences of a murder in June 1996 that shocked the entire nation and left the door open for them to become major players in the west of the city.

On the 26th of that month, crime reporter Veronica Guerin was shot dead as she sat in her red Opel sports car at traffic lights in Clondalkin, around five miles from the area "served" by Sugg and Coates. The murder was carried out by a gang controlled by Blanchardstown mobster John Gilligan, who had built up a massive drugs importation and supply network in Dublin.

There was a massive public outcry about the callous murder and Gilligan became the Garda's target number one. He was later tried, but acquitted, for Ms Guerin's murder — although he was jailed for 20 years for drugs importation.

But the Garda investigation dismantled Gilligan's drugs supply network and left a major gap in the Blanchardstown area.

That was a gap that Sugg and Coates were only too happy to fill. "They saw their chance to make serious money and went for it," one officer said. "With Gilligan and most of his people out of the way, there was a vacuum in relation to the supply of cannabis in large parts of the DMR West [the policing division that includes the Blanchardstown area]. Sugg and Coates saw the possibility taking over from Gilligan and started ramping up their activities."

And, for at least one rival, the decision by Sugg and Coates to up their game would have fatal consequences.

Paschal Boland didn't frighten easily.

The 43-year-old, from Ashcroft Court in Mulhuddart, west Dublin, showed no fear when the Westies came for him. It was late 1998 and Coates and Sugg were on his tail.

They were unhappy that Boland, a well-known drug dealer in the Finglas area, was trying to extend his market and move in on their patch. Boland sent his network of street dealers into Blanchardstown, where the Westies had been holding court for several years. And, like the best legitimate entrepreneur, Boland knew that there was only one way he could lure customers from the grip of the Westies: he undercut them.

If the Westies were selling heroin for £20 a fix, he charged £15. For junkies who have to have eight or nine hits a day that is a huge amount of money. Before long, money talked and Boland was carving out huge swathes of the Westies' Blanchardstown patch as his own.

Sugg and Coates, suddenly found themselves under pressure in their own backyard. They knew they had to act.

In December of that year, Sugg and Coates assaulted one of Boland's street dealers and gave him a mobile phone. They told him to bring the mobile phone to Boland. He did as he was told and, several hours later, the phone rang. It was Shane Coates, and he had a simple message for Boland: stop dealing drugs on the Westies' turf or he was a dead man.

In that instant, Boland had a decision to make. He could have decided to back off, to make his money somewhere else, somewhere where the Westies had no reach. Or he could decide to face them down. In a heartbeat, he chose the latter.

Almost as soon as Coates had stopped talking, Boland started laughing. He told Coates that he and Sugg were nobodies, that he was not afraid of them and if they wanted war, they would get a war. And then he hung up.

A few weeks later, the Westies showed him they were far from nobodies.

Just after 9pm on Wednesday, January 27, 1999, Pascal Boland pulled his car into the driveway of his home.

As soon as he got out of his vehicle, a waiting gunman pounced. The assassin walked towards Boland, his face hidden by a balaclava, a semi-automatic pistol in his hand. Although his identity was hidden, detectives later established the hitman was Stephen Sugg.

Boland, just a few feet away, knew he was finished. He couldn't fight him and he couldn't outrun him. All he could do was beg.

By coincidence, just as the killing was about to unfold, Boland's partner Lisa Quinn was looking out of the upstairs front window. She saw Boland pleading, in vain, with Sugg to spare him his life.

"I heard Pascal say, 'Don't shoot me, don't shoot me' at the same time as the shots," she said seven years later at his inquest.

But the gunman ignored his pleas. At point-blank range, the gunman pumped up to seven shots into his body. As Boland slumped, fatally injured to the floor, the masked Sugg ran off. Boland was rushed to the nearby James Connolly Memorial Hospital, but was declared dead an hour later.

The Westies had drawn their first blood. Nobody could touch them now. They owned Blanchardstown.

With Boland out of the way, Sugg and Coates spent much of 1999 and the year 2000 trying to widen their empire. They knew that, with Blanchardstown under their control and nobody brave enough to take them on, they could now become the biggest dealers in Dublin.

By this stage, cocaine was becoming increasingly popular as the fledgling Celtic Tiger saw more young people with enough cash to use the party drug at the weekends. The Westies knew that they could make a fortune by selling coke, cannabis and heroin throughout the city.

But to bring in the large-scale drugs shipments that would mark them as serious players, Sugg and Coates needed access to significant amounts of cash. They knew that they would need to buy consignments from major dealers in Spain for several hundred thousand pounds before they could turn that into sales worth several million in Dublin.

For example, a kilo of cocaine sold in Dublin is worth some €70,000 on the streets. But it is bought in Spain by smugglers for around €25,000, depending on bulk sales. It is then cut, or diluted, into three kilos for sale on the streets. That means that a €25,000 outlay in Spain brings a cash turnover in Dublin of some €210,000.

With all costs taken out of that, the gang bosses probably earn €70,000 per every €25,000 outlay — massive profits. But the money for the consignments has to be paid in advance, and if the drugs are seized, that's the purchaser's problem. The cartels in Spain still have to be paid. That all meant the Westies needed hundreds of thousands of euro to buy their drugs — and they knew a simple way to get their hands on the cash.

The ranks of their gang were, by the early months of the year 2000, swollen to around 50 criminals. Most were from Blanchardstown and Finglas and many of them were seasoned gangsters. One speciality the gang boasted was what British criminals call blagging, or armed robberies. Coates and Sugg used that expertise to carry out several high-profile heists — money they used to buy drugs in Spain.

It's thought the Westies stole more than €1m in the period 1999 to 2001. This haul, coupled with the murder of Pascal Boland, made the Westies one of the main targets of the Garda in the city.

"Something had to be done," one office active at the time said. "They were extremely active in the DMR West [Blanchardstown and Finglas] and were causing Garda management serious problems. They were carrying out robbery after robbery and were very dangerous."

Garda bosses started fighting back in December 2001 with Operation Discovery, an effort to crack down on the number of security van heists in the greater Dublin area. After 27 in 2001 alone. Investigators believed the Westies were involved in as many as half of them. Some 10 of the 27 happened in the Westies' Blanchardstown stomping ground.

Discovery was old-fashioned, in-your-face policing. Armed detectives, including officers from Blanchardstown, Special Branch and the National Bureau of Criminal Investigation, not only provided escorts to the security vans, but also carried out snap vehicle checkpoints in areas where the Westies were active.

They repeatedly stopped and searched major players in the Westies gang, including Coates, Sugg, his brother Bernard "Verb" Sugg and two brothers Mark and Andrew Glennon. "These five were the main targets of Discovery in Blanchardstown," one source said. "They were the leaders and key lieutenants of the Westies. We knew we had to crack down hard on the leadership of the gang, and that is what we did."

The five were stopped at checkpoints and while they were walking on the street every week for several months. Their homes were repeatedly raided and they were put under intensive, overt surveillance.

The Criminal Assets Bureau was also taking a keen interest in Sugg and Coates. There, specialist detectives were analysing their assets and working out how much each man had made from the drugs trade. They would later be handed hefty tax demands.

Within a few months, the operation started to pay off: the number of armed robberies reduced to barely a trickle. The Westies found it hard to move without being stopped and hassled by armed gardai. "There is no doubt that Discovery had a major effect on the gang's capabilities," a senior officer confirmed. "They were under serious pressure by the middle of 2002."

The dramatic reduction in robberies was an undoubted success for the operation. But those successes led to tensions with the gang — tensions that would have horrific consequences for several families in west Dublin.

And they were tensions that would, ultimately lead to the grisly deaths in Spain of Sugg and Coates.

By February 2002, the tensions were beginning to rip the Westies apart. The two Glennon brothers, particularly, were unhappy with the leadership of Sugg and Coates. They felt they were not getting their fair share of the proceeds of the drug dealing and robberies.

They wanted a bigger slice of the cake and knew exactly what to do — in the age-old way of the gangster, they decided to mount a coup. They were about to turn on the leadership of the Westies.

For more than five years, Sugg and Coates had been on an upward trajectory in gangland Dublin. They murdered Pascal Boland to show that no-one could muscle in on their patch; they terrified and tortured junkies who owed them just a few quid: they caused gardai serious headaches with their drug-dealing and robberies. Their ascent to the top of the tree in Irish crime seemed unstoppable.

But they failed to take into account one simple factor — members of gangs don't know the meaning of the word loyalty. Perhaps their growing reputation as the hard men of west Dublin clouded their judgement, perhaps they naively thought their gang was rock solid behind them; perhaps they believed nobody would have the bottle to take them on.

Either way, they were blind to the Glennons' efforts to take away their empire until it was too late. Gardai believe the Glennons spent several months plotting to take out Coates and Sugg before making their first move in April 2002.

Just after midnight on Monday, April 15, Bernard "Verb" Sugg, who was 21 at the time, was standing at an open area of ground close to Corduff Shopping Centre when one of the Glennons came for him.

Armed with a sawn-off shotgun and a mask covering his face, the gunman drew a bead on Verb from just a few feet away. He fired one shot right at him before fleeing. Verb slumped to the ground, a hole in his stomach.

He was rushed to the nearby James Connolly Memorial Hospital, where he was treated for his wounds. Miraculously, he survived the incident — the wound was only superficial. But gardai had no doubt that this was an attempt to kill Verb Sugg — it's likely he survived because the shotgun pellets were smaller, and less lethal than the ammunition normally used.

Sugg got lucky that day. But gardai knew the attack meant a new chapter was unfolding in the Westies' saga as they turned on each other. Officers did not have to wait more than a few months for the next incident.

In October 2002, Stephen Sugg was relaxing in his house in Corduff when the Glennons came for him. When they tried to kill his brother, they used a shotgun — this time they had brought something much more powerful with them. The Ingram MAC-10 is a US-built submachine pistol and is one of the most deadly weapons in the world. It fires 1,100 rounds per minute, which means it effectively delivers a sheet of bullets capable of cutting a person in half. This was the weapon the Glennons used in their latest onslaught on the Suggs.

A gunmen drove up to the house just before 10pm. He

stepped out of the car, paused for a few seconds and let loose. The gun had been set to fully automatic and when the gunman pressed the trigger, more than 40 bullets were spat out of the muzzle in less than a second. The recoil from the gun was so fierce that the gunman immediately lost control of the weapon and the bullets started flying everywhere. Several kids lived in the houses close to Sugg's property and it was a miracle that none of them was hurt. Most of the bullets missed Sugg's home and he was uninjured.

But he was left severely shaken by the attack and knew the Glennons were out to murder him. It was all getting too much for Sugg now. His own gang was turning against him, gardai were cracking down on the gang and the Criminal Assets Bureau had slapped both he and Coates with tax bills for more than €100,000.

He made an instant decision, telling only his close pal Coates — he was getting out of Dodge. Within a week of the shooting, Stephen Sugg got on a plane at Dublin Airport and flew south to Alicante, on the south east coast of Spain.

He had contacts there already with other criminals and planned to stay in nearby Torrevieja for several months. Sources say he believed gardai were close to arresting him and charging him with several of the armed robberies investigated under Operation Discovery. But, even more importantly, he got out of Blanchardstown because he really believed that the Glennons were going to murder him.

Coates, on the other hand, decided to stay in Ireland. He was not afraid of the Garda and was definitely not frightened by the Glennons. He decided to stay and fight. And, rather than keeping his head down, he kept up his drugs trade despite the Glennons' efforts. He also hit on a plan to get the firearms he desperately needed to take his war to his new enemies. It was a plan that would have fatal consequences for both him and Sugg.

In May 2003, Coates decided to target a licensed gun dealer living in Balbriggan, north Co Dublin. At 1.30am on May 16, Coates and three associates burst into the family home beside the dealer's business.

A gun was held to the man's head and he was ordered to turn off the house alarm. The gang, all wearing balaclavas, man-handled the family into a room where they tied them up and locked them in. The raiders took 14 sporting firearms, cash and jewellery. The family managed to free themselves eventually and broke out of the room at 3.45am to raise the alarm.

"It was a job well-organised," Detective Superintendent Michael Hoare conceded. "The family were badly traumatised and shook up after their ordeal. They were held for a good hour, maybe two."

While the family were recovering, Coates and his associates were lying low at an isolated cottage in Virginia, Co Cavan. They were getting ready to use the weapons for more robberies and attacks on the Glennons. But gardai had other plans.

Two days later, gardai received intelligence that Coates and others were in the house in Cavan and elite officers were sent to the scene. National Surveillance Unit officers began a secret surveillance operation, constantly watching the cottage from nearby fields. They were tasked with monitoring the suspects before the Garda SWAT team, the Emergency Response Unit, stormed the property.

But before the ERU could arrive on the scene, a local uniformed garda on patrol in the area thought he saw suspicious activity in the house and — unarmed — went to investigate.

When Coates saw him coming down the driveway, he knew he had to act. He pulled out a shotgun and ordered the garda not to move. The garda tried to struggle with the gang, but he was outnumbered.

Coates and his pals were bundling the officer into the boot of a car when the NSU acted to save his life. An undercover garda emerged from the bushes and, pistol in hand, ordered Coates to put down the shotgun.

But instead of obeying the detective's order, Coates raised his weapon and fired at him. The blast missed the detective but he fired back, hitting Coates in the leg.

In the ensuing shootout, Coates managed to drive off in his

van and escape across the nearby border into the North. The PSNI later found blood-soaked bandages in a hotel room in Co Fermanagh, with Coates's DNA on them. Detectives quickly established that Coates had forced a local doctor to stitch up his leg wound hours after he was shot. He then hid out in the North for several days before heading to Britain on a ferry. From there, he got to a London airport and joined Sugg in Alicante.

Both men were now exiled from Dublin. Both men knew they could never return home: if the gardai didn't get them, the Glennons would.

It was time for them to start a new life in Spain.

Within weeks of the Virginia shootout, Sugg and Coates had rented an apartment in Orihuela Costa, close to Torrevieja, and had brought their partners out to live with them. Irish under-world sources in Torrevieja told *The Star* that the pair became well-known in the area.

"They had a few contacts here and they quickly started mingling with other Irish criminals," a source revealed. "Sugg and Coates would have been well-known here amongst other Irish criminals and they had a bit of a reputation as hard men. There were no major incidents in the first few months that they were here, but people were certainly wary of them."

The pair were regularly seen enjoying bars, pubs and restaurants in Torrevieja, La Zenia and Playa Flamenca. But they weren't just there for the sun. Sugg and Coates needed money and there was only one thing they were good at: crime.

Both men decided, in the summer of 2003, to establish a smuggling route for cannabis from Spain to their associates in Ireland. Every year, tonnes of cannabis are smuggled in to Spain from nearby Morocco. From there, the massive consignments are broken down into smaller batches and sent to gangs in other countries.

The Westies quickly established links with drugs suppliers in Alicante and began sending their own cannabis back to Ireland. They got it in any way they could, primarily by paying Irish people going back home to bring a few kilos with them, or by smuggling larger consignments via crooked lorry drivers.

But they also hit on the ingenious plan of sending half-kilo batches by post. They used addresses of ordinary, unsuspecting citizens and intercepted the parcels before they reached their destination, sending one of their couriers to hang around the address waiting for the postman or parcel delivery van.

When the parcel arrived, the lurking courier told the postman that it was his parcel and made off with the drugs.

Gardai believe the Westies sent in several million euro worth of the drug before the scam was uncovered in December 2003. But by then it was too late: Sugg and Coates had made a fortune from the scam and were enjoying themselves with the profits in Torrevieja.

But their fun would soon come to an abrupt end in the most violent of ways.

On January 31, 2004, Sugg and Coates told their partners that they were heading off for a meeting and would be back within a few hours. They were never seen again.

The girls started to become anxious when they hadn't heard from them in a few hours. It simply wasn't like their boys not to stay in contact with them, no matter what they were up to. Early the next morning, the partners woke up, terrified, to find a masked man in their apartment. They screamed and he ran off with one of their handbags, escaping in Sugg's car. But it was all the confirmation they needed: something had happened to their boys.

Spanish cops were alerted and they in turn contacted the Garda in Dublin, with both police forces trawling their intelligence assets for information.

But no-one seemed to know anything. The pair had simply vanished in to thin air. Gardai didn't know if they had been abducted, murdered, or had merely faked their own deaths. "There was a strong theory at the start that they had decided to do a runner and go somewhere like Morocco to start afresh," one officer said. "It was taken quite seriously, because there was just no intelligence out there. No-one could say if they were alive or dead."

But the men's families were convinced from day one that something terrible had happened to them. Christian Coates is Shane's brother and a respected academic researcher at Trinity College Dublin. Within a few days of their disappearance, he said: "I think they might have gone to meet somebody some place, that they might have been trapped. The type of people Shane knows, you'd never know what might happen. They are either in some police cell in Spain after being arrested and having given false names or else something serious has happened to them. We are convinced this is not a hoax."

Spanish police spent several days combing the Costa Blanca looking for any sign of the men — or even of freshly-dug secret graves. But they found nothing.

After a few weeks, the search was officially scaled down and they were treated by Spanish cops as just two more missing people in a country where thousands disappear every year. As 2004 went by and the families woke up to New Year's Day in Dublin in 2005, there were was still no sign of the men.

But while Spanish cops were content to let the matter rest, detectives back in Dublin were feverishly trying to get to the bottom of the mystery. The main theory shortly after the disappearance was that the Westies had tried to muscle in on the operations of one of the dozens of Russian mafia gangs that have flooded in to Alicante in recent years.

But in early 2005, the gardai got their first, tiny, break.

Word reached detectives in Blanchardstown that local sources there believed the Westies had been murdered by Irish criminals in Torrevieja. Officers spent months trying to eke out as much information as they could from the informants. At the end of the year, officers were told that the pair had been shot in the head and buried under a building, somewhere in the Alicante area.

In January 2006, they were given one, tentative, address and officers from the Garda National Drugs Unit were dispatched to take part in a dig with members of the Spanish Guardia Civil. They spent several days excavating a site in the Catral area — but they came up with nothing.

Dejected, the GNDU detectives headed back to Dublin. But their colleagues in Blanchardstown refused to give up and kept working their informants. That hard work paid off in late June, when another address was provided — this time a warehouse in an industrial estate in the town.

Again, the GNDU detectives, led by Chief Superintendent Cormac Gordon, took the flight to Alicante, where they met their Spanish colleagues once more. And again, they watched as the Guardia Civil began an excavation operation.

But, unlike before, this dig produced the results the police had been hoping for. Within a few minutes of digging, the Spanish officers hit pay dirt.

They found two large rolls of plastic buried under six feet of concrete and two feet of soil. They carefully opened the sheeting and found skeletal remains. Both had been shot in the head. Even without formal identification, the gardai knew it was them. Some 18 months after the pair disappeared, the mystery of the Westies had been solved — now all gardai had to do was catch the killers.

Within hours of the discovery, cops raided a villa close to Torrevieja's main hospital and arrested Irish gangster 'Fat' Tony Armstrong over the deaths. He had been renting the warehouse under which the bodies were found.

Armstrong, who was then 32, was originally from Finglas and had been living in Torrevieja for several years. He was on the run from gardai who wanted to question him about the 1998 robbery of a bank in Phibsboro, north Dublin — but was keeping a low profile in Spain. That was, until he was arrested over the Westies' deaths.

Armstrong was told he was being formally investigated in relation to the murder of both men but was never charged. Instead, he was held in custody for more than a year while the investigation continued. Back home in Ireland, gardai got DNA samples from Sugg and Coates relatives and, in early 2007, the remains were formally identified as the missing men.

That July, the two were finally flown home to be buried. Coates was the first to be interred: he was laid to rest just six hours after his coffin landed at Dublin Airport. Two days later Sugg was laid to rest in the same grave as his brother Verb, who had been shot dead in Blanchardstown in August 2003.

The men who carried out that killing, Mark and Andrew Glennon, were murdered in 2005. They too were buried together. There were no winners in this gangland war.

But the saga had a happier ending for at least one man. Some 13 months after he was arrested, Tony Armstrong walked free from prison in Alicante. Spanish law states that if a suspect has been held for a year without charge, he must either be released on bail or told he was to be prosecuted.

The Spanish had no evidence against him and set him free. In 2010, he was finally told that the case against him was being shelved due to a lack of evidence. Spanish cops had demanded that gardai tell them where they got their intelligence that the Westies were buried in the property he rented — but detectives in Ireland refused. They did not want to jeopardise the safety of their informants. The stand-off meant that there was no evidence against Armstrong and he walked free.

In May 2010, *The Star* tracked him down to a pub in Torrevieja — where he was in bullish form. He insisted he played no hand in the killing of two of Ireland's most dangerous criminals. He said: "There never was evidence and there couldn't be evidence for the simple reason that I had f**king nothing do with it. I am innocent. I had nothing to do with it and that's that."

With that, Armstrong turned his back on us, went back into the pub — and started the rest of his life.

KELLY ANN CORCORAN:
A family torn apart

EARLY on the afternoon of Sunday, September 28, 2008, a small group of Irish men and women walked through the main square of Malaga. The city and its hinterland, on the Costa del Sol in south east Spain, is a Mecca for tens of thousands of Irish tourists every year. From there, most of them drive the 40 odd miles to the main resorts of Torremolinos, Marbella and Benalmadena.

But this 15-strong Irish group was different. They weren't in Spain for the sun, sangria or sand. They had no interest in the area's famous nightlife. Instead, they had made the trek from the north east of Ireland to finally see justice for a pretty young woman they all loved and missed.

They had been waiting more than eight years for the possibility of securing justice for mum-of-two Kelly Ann Corcoran — and now that wait was almost at an end.

There were only a few excruciating hours left before her family and friends, who had kept her memory alive ever since she fell from the balcony of a Marbella hotel in early 2000, would sit in a Malaga courtroom and watch her widower Dermot McArdle go on trial for her murder.

They had all kept their counsel ever since Kelly Ann's sudden and shocking death. They never once spoke to the media who had been chasing the story since her death and were in no mood to break that habit now. With the trial so close, they refused point blank to talk to journalists who approached them in the city centre that Sunday afternoon.

Instead, they just walked around the historic town centre for a few hours, trying to kill time.

It was no struggle for them — they had been killing time ever since Kelly Ann, a mum to two young boys, fell from the fourth floor of the Melia Don Pepe Hotel while on the first day of a week-long holiday with her husband on February 11, 2000.

They spent agonising days waiting for Kelly Ann's body to come home after she died; they spent months waiting for the Spanish police to finish their inquiry into her death; they waited years as McArdle fought the Spanish authorities tooth and nail in their bid to extradite him to Spain to face trial over the death.

Around 20 miles away, the man they blamed for Kelly Ann's death was also killing time. But while the Corcorans and their friends were waiting with anticipation, Dermot Michael McArdle was more than likely dreading what was going to happen the next day.

McArdle, who was aged 39 on that September evening, was staying at an apartment in the Fuengirola area, with his two kids from his marriage to Kelly Ann, Mark and Paul.

His new partner Clare Dollard was also with him, as were his parents. But, even though he was surrounded by his loved ones, he was essentially alone. He knew that the events of the next week — how long his trial was expected to last — would have a massive bearing on the rest of his life.

If the jury believed him, that his wife fell from the balcony accidentally, despite his efforts to save her, he would be a free man and the weight on his shoulders for the last eight years would finally be eased.

But if the jury accepted the prosecution's claim that he caused Kelly Ann's death during an argument, he would be labelled a wife-killer for the rest of his life.

He would also face the prospect of being locked up in a Spanish prison for as many as 14 years. Spanish prosecutors were also demanding that McArdle pay €200,000 to the family of Kelly Ann Corcoran. The stakes were massively high for him — and he was simply not prepared to lose.

He had fought frantically against the prosecution for more than eight years. There was no way he would give up now.

McArdle had been made aware that Spanish cops suspected he killed Kelly Ann within days of the tragedy and had been fighting an increasingly desperate rear-guard ever since.

Within weeks of Kelly Ann's death, two Spanish detectives flew to his native Dundalk, Co Louth, as part of their probe. But they had no powers of arrest in Ireland and he stubbornly chose to ignore them, refusing on legal advice to even meet them.

Eventually, after an exhaustive investigation, the Spanish authorities found enough evidence to convince a prosecutor in Marbella that McArdle should be charged with the 28-year-old's murder.

The judge ordered his arrest and charge in October 2001 — 20 months after her death. Spanish cops quickly submitted an extradition request to the Irish authorities and a judge in Dublin ordered McArdle's arrest on foot of that warrant.

Although often complex, such extraditions are usually completed within two or three months. But there was nothing usual about the McArdle murder case.

The meat factory manager, who comes from a well-known family in Dundalk, fought an expensive and unprecedented legal war against his extradition and prosecution that went to the highest court in not one, but two countries.

He battled the extradition every possible step in the Irish legal system, ending up in the Supreme Court — the final arbiter of justice in Ireland. That would, normally, have been the end of the affair — but this was no normal case.

When McArdle, known to be hugely stubborn and arrogant by people who grew up with him, lost in Ireland, he changed tactics and picked another battlefield.

This time, he took the war to Spain, trying to have his case thrown out at every available opportunity.

In the end, he not only lost every battle, but finally lost his desperate war. But the Corcoran family would have to wait an incredible 91 months — almost eight years — for him to be brought to account.

The justice they so desperately craved was agonisingly close — they could almost touch it. Now all they had to do was wait a few hours.

It was supposed to be a holiday to get away from it all. Early on the morning of February 11, 2000, meat factory manager Dermot McArdle, his 28-year-old wife Kelly Ann Corcoran and their three-year-old son Mark drove from their home in Wheaton Hall, Drogheda, Co Louth, to Dublin Airport.

The couple's youngest son, Paul, was under two and he was being looked after by relatives as the rest of the family jetted off to Malaga on an Aer Lingus flight.

When they landed, they drove for about an hour until they reached the five-star Hotel Melia Don Pepe in the centre of Marbella, the most luxurious sun resort on the Costa del Sol.

The couple and Mark moved into room 421 of the prestigious hotel, with a balcony overlooking the swimming pool and dining area. They stayed in the room for a short while, before heading out to Marbella for a few hours.

They walked along the beach, went to a bar and then headed to an Italian restaurant for an early dinner before returning to the hotel.

What happened next is the stuff of nightmares. Only two people know the full truth. One of them, Kelly, who is dead and can't give her version of events. The other, McArdle, who consistently proclaimed his innocence for eight years — but in the end, was simply not believed by a jury.

Either way, one thing is known for sure. That evening,

at around 7pm, Kelly Ann fell around 20 metres from the balcony of the room, landing hard on the ground and suffering horrific head injuries.

She was rushed to a local hospital, as McArdle informed her devastated parents Ted and Bridie in Dundalk.

Spanish police immediately began an investigation and spoke to several people at the hotel.

Two days later she died in hospital — after doctors told him there was no hope for her. She had suffered a brain haemorrhage. She also had broken bones in her left leg and foot, as well as suffering wounds to her head, chin, shoulders and upper body.

McArdle donated all her organs — except her eyes.

A few days later, Kelly Ann's body was flown home on a private jet owned by beef baron Larry Goodman, who employed McArdle at the time.

What happened next is etched in Ted Corcoran's memory. He, along with several other members, had flown out to Marbella once they heard the news and flew back on the same jet with McArdle.

McArdle brought him aside and implied that Kelly Ann did not fall accidentally over the balcony — she threw herself over it in a suicide attempt.

"He told me that he and Kelly Ann had an argument and that Kelly Ann did not mean to do anything. I did not like what I was hearing at that time — I pushed him away," Mr Corcoran recalled.

He also said McArdle looked cool as a cucumber just a day after the fall. "He did not look sad — he was cool as a cucumber. He did not show any remorse. It seemed like it was a party for him," Mr Corcoran added.

Worse was to come when they brought Kelly Ann's body home.

One of Mr Goodman's drivers was waiting for them at Dublin Airport in a Mercedes and drove them back to Dundalk.

Mr Corcoran recalled: "He came out with me in the

Mercedes and he asked the driver to keep the car running, that he was not going to be long. The driver stayed in the car and he came with me into the house. There was a lot of people there, this was like a wake. He maybe stayed six minutes and he was gone. He stayed six minutes. He got in the car and was gone and he never came near us."

The Corcorans were horrified. They had just lost their daughter, McArdle had just lost his wife — yet he spent just six minutes in the family home when her body was returned.

But it got even worse. They continued to be appalled by his behaviour immediately after Kelly Ann's death.

When Kelly Ann was lying in state in an Irish funeral home, her sister Caroline placed a hand on her head and McArdle told her: "Get your f***ing hand off her head." Then, on the day of the funeral, he put a fist to her face.

He gave her a prayer for the Mass and told her with his fist on her face: "If you are going to cry, don't do it, I will get someone else."

Mrs Moran also alleged that the family had to fight and plead with him to see Kelly Ann in her coffin before her funeral. And Ted Corcoran said he was horrified by McArdle's demeanour on the day of the funeral. "During the funeral he never sat with us," he recalled.

Then, several months after her death, the Corcorans received a hammer blow from the most unexpected of quarters — Kelly Ann's own son, Mark.

Mark, who was in the room when his mother fell from the balcony, was in a car one day with his aunt Caroline, Kelly Ann's still heartbroken sister. He started talking.

Caroline could simply not believe what she was hearing. "Mark got very distressed," she said. "He said 'Daddy was a bold boy. Daddy hit mummy and pushed mammy and pushed her down.'" She became upset and asked a friend in the car, Niamh Hegarty, if she had heard what he said.

When she said no, she asked Mark to repeat what he had said — and he did. It chimed with something Mark had said to Peter Moran, Caroline's husband, a day after Kelly Ann had died. He, too, was aghast, especially as McArdle had told him at the Marbella hospital as Kelly Ann fought for her life that she had thrown herself over the balcony.

"I could not believe what I was hearing and Dermot had told me in the room in the hospital that Kelly Ann did not mean it and that she threw herself over the balcony. I did not know whether Dermot was right and the child misunderstood. I was confused," Mr Moran said.

While the Corcorans were becoming increasingly confused about what happened on the balcony, the Spanish police were becoming increasingly interested — and wanted to quiz McArdle.

But there was only one problem — he was back in Ireland and Spanish law has no writ there. They needed the help of the Gardai. In March 2000, just over a month after Kelly Ann's death, two detectives travelled from Malaga to carry out inquiries in Ireland. A senior garda, now assistant Commissioner John O'Mahoney, helped draw up a list of 33 questions the Spaniards wanted to put to him. But the whole trip was in vain. McArdle point blank refused to see them, on legal advice from a barrister who is now one of Ireland's top judges.

Barry White — who was the judge in the Joe O'Reilly and Brian Kearney murder trials — was a respected senior counsel at the time cops wanted to interview McArdle in 2000.

McArdle said his solicitor got advice from the barrister, who said he shouldn't make a statement to the police — because he had already done so in Spain.

However, despite his reticence, Spanish police believed they had enough evidence for him to be charged — evidence that would become stunningly clear eight years later.

They then started a lengthy extradition process and, despite numerous appeals by McArdle, he became the first person ever to be extradited from Ireland under the new European arrest warrant.

That law, which came into effect in 2001, made it easier for EU member states to send people to each other's jurisdictions to stand trial. In effect, all a foreign state had to do was send over the relevant paperwork, provided the extradition was for the purpose of a charge.

McArdle took his opposition to the extradition request as far as he could in Ireland when he mounted a Supreme Court challenge in 2005. But on November 4 of that year, the court threw out his fight and he was put on a flight to Spain.

That, incredibly, was nowhere near the end of the saga. A judge in Marbella allowed him out on bail and he started working in a factory in San Carles De La Rapita, near Barcelona in the north of the country – but 600 miles from Malaga, where he was due to stand trial.

Bizarrely, he was then allowed back home to live in Ireland, until his court date was fixed. That decision, in the end, allowed him to live in his native Dundalk for a full three years.

After he failed in the Irish courts, McArdle — who was by now being sued for more than €200,000 over unpaid fees by the Dundalk solicitors he used in the Irish challenge — took the fight to Spain. He launched legal attempts on at least three occasions to have the charge against him thrown out.

He wanted the case dismissed, arguing that he would not receive a fair trial. But, on each occasion, he lost his legal gamble.

By the start of 2008, he was running out of time. On March 12 of that year, he went on trial at Dundalk District Court accused of assaulting one of his nephews — the son of Caroline, Kelly Ann's sister.

The court acquitted him of that charge, but it also heard that he had lost his final appeal against the murder trial going ahead in Malaga. He had nowhere left to run, nowhere left to hide. Now he would have to convince a Spanish court that he was innocent of Kelly Ann's murder.

McArdle strode confidently into court number 4 of the

Andalusian Provincial court complex on the outskirts of Malaga city just after 10am on Tuesday, September 30, 2008.

The trial had been chalked down to start the previous day, but it had been delayed by 24 hours. He walked past the Corcorans and Kelly Ann's friends without even acknowledging him. These were people with whom, before Kelly Ann's death, he was extremely close. But now, he didn't even look at them. The feeling was more than mutual.

Anyone who has ever been to an Irish trial will know that the way we do our criminal cases is hugely different from most of the European mainland.

In Ireland, like the UK, we use the Common Law system, which sees prosecution state its case, then the defence mounts its case. In the end, it is all down to which side the judge, or jury believes.

If the prosecution case is accepted, the accused is convicted. If the defence manage to weaken the prosecution case enough, the accused is acquitted.

Spain, however, runs a totally different system. And when trial judge Fernando Gonzalez opened the proceedings that September morning, he was explicit, saying: "We are here to find the truth, nothing more."

It was not a question of one side attacking the other, it was a question of the jury listening to all the evidence and making its own, objective, decision. It wasn't a case, for example, of the jury accepting part of the prosecution case, but rejecting others. The jury was free to do as it chose — but, crucially, was expected to issue a statement after its verdict, explaining fully its reasons for the findings it made.

In Ireland during a murder trial, the first thing the jury hears is called the opener — the initial statement by the prosecution, in which the main claims are aired. They are also told what evidence they will hear — and that it will convince them of the accused's guilt. The trial then begins for real.

Spain, however, could not be more different. The first thing that happened in McArdle's trial was that he was asked to take to the witness stand and give his version of events. He took his chance with some gusto.

McArdle told the court how he, Kelly Ann and young Mark, who was then just three, spent a few hours in Marbella before heading back to their hotel.

He admitted that he had had two incidents with Kelly Ann — one moments before she fell and one an hour previously.

The first row happened after they had gone for an Italian meal in Marbella, just hours after booking in to their hotel for a week-long holiday before he started a new job.

They left their second son Paul, who was only two then, back in Ireland with relatives because he was too young to travel, he said. He said they met two English couples in a pub — and with the men he had gone for a kick about with Mark, while Kelly Ann stayed in the bar with the women.

A few minutes later he started talking to the female bar owner about good restaurants and lost sight of Mark, he said.

He then looked up and Mark was standing with Kelly Ann on a bank beside the pub. "I proceeded immediately to go up towards both of them," he said.

"Kelly Ann started to give out to me that I should have been giving more attention to my child and not be talking to any ladies — but she didn't know what I was talking about. I had never known Kelly Ann to be jealous, but she told me not to be talking to any women."

He said she and his wife walked, apart, back to the hotel where Kelly Ann continued complaining to him about talking to the woman. He said he then walked up to the hotel room, expecting Kelly Ann to be there — but she wasn't.

He and Mark spent an hour looking for Kelly Ann before heading back to the hotel — and when he went to the room she was inside, he said.

"She had her money and travellers' cheques in her hand — she was going to cash the travellers' cheques. I asked her to stay in the room," he said. "We had been up very early that morning, at 5.30am, and we needed to rest and we had enough to drink.

"Kelly Ann said she wanted to go back out for more drink.

I said we needed to go to bed."

Just at that, he said, he saw Mark climbing on the balcony and he and Kelly Ann raced over to rescue him.

But, he said, she was running at speed and she stumbled at the entrance to the balcony — and went head first over it.

"She stumbled and she went to put her hands out to save herself. But she missed the handrail because it was so low. Her body took her over the balcony. I went to grab her and I ended up grabbing her left arm. I started calling for help," he said.

When he was asked how long he struggled to keep Kelly Ann from falling, he replied: "A couple of minutes. Both my feet were off the ground and I was shouting for help."

He said he then lost his strength and couldn't hold her anymore — so she plunged 40 feet to the ground. "I ran to the elevator to go down to find where Kelly Ann was. She was lying part on a small wall, the rest on the grass. I stayed with her until the ambulance arrived."

It was a bravura, but vicious, performance. He came across as a loving husband, who was aghast that his wife wanted to continue drinking instead of looking after her own child.

Even after her death, he sullied her name. She came across as a woman more interested in booze than her baby. Even now, more than two years later, family and friends are still devastated when they think about his evidence.

He left the stand after around two hours, looking happy with himself. But what happened next must have destroyed the cockiness he was undoubtedly feeling.

Frail English pensioner Roy Haines walked slowly, but confidently, to the witness stand. He had been, with his wife, in the adjacent room when Kelly Ann fell. His evidence was short — but stunningly to the point.

"It was such a horrifying incident that we did our best to get it out of our minds," Mr Haines told Judge Fernando Gonzalez. "All I heard was a lot of arguing from the next door bedroom and or balcony. Through a window we briefly saw the gentleman [McArdle] next door lift the girl over his head on the balcony. I told him to put her down and went inside and shut the door.

"The next thing that we heard was the shouts of 'help, help'."

Stunned, the defence team asked him why he had never made such a claim to the police, whom he merely told that Kelly Ann was motionless as McArdle held her over the balcony. "They didn't ask me," was his curt reply.

The next day a horrible drama took place that, briefly, united McArdle and the Corcorans in genuine upset.

Little Mark, who was alleged to have said as a three-year-old that he saw his father Dermot McArdle push Kelly Ann in the hotel room, was called to give evidence.

As he was a minor, the public and media were asked to leave the courtroom and he gave his evidence in private.

Members of the public and the media outside court number four heard the female interpreter in the court scream — and a few moments later, members of the Guardia Civil police rushed inside. It then became clear that Mark had collapsed and some of the Corcoran family — who were outside the court — started crying. Three paramedics then rushed into the court but the boy was already being treated by medics who were there to give evidence.

Half an hour later the case resumed and Judge Gonzalez said the child would not be giving anymore evidence, but the distressing incident showed to everyone just how tense and stressful a time it was for all the participants involved.

But before the court finished for the day there was even more drama when a sister of McArdle claimed in court that Kelly Ann's father, Ted, said he knew what his daughter was like when she had drink taken — as she lay fighting for her life following her fall from the hotel room balcony.

Theresa McArdle claimed Ted Corcoran made the comment to her and Dermot in a Marbella hospital when her brother was explaining to him how she had fallen off the balcony trying to save little Mark.

"Mr Corcoran kept saying 'Son, I know, I know what she's like with drink in her'," she said. The Corcoran family, including Ted, reacted furiously in court to the claim. Mr Corcoran exclaimed: "Oh my God," while a woman shouted "No" — and several other family members began crying.

The next day was crucial in the case. And evidence heard that day from elite police officers gave the Corcorans a groundswell of hope that McArdle was bound to be convicted of murder — only for their hearts to be broken a few hours later.

A Spanish Guardia Civil forensics expert was called to give evidence — and quite simply demolished McArdle's claim that Kelly Ann tripped and fell over the balcony as she ran to save Mark.

"It is totally impossible. It is scientifically impossible," the senior officer said. And he then produced the killer quote. Kelly Ann would have to have been faster than Olympic sprint champion Usain Bolt for McArdle's version of events to be believable, he said. In other words, what McArdle was claiming was simply incredible. "To be correct, the woman would have had to be moving at 12 metres per second," the officer said. "At that speed, she would be running the 100 metres in less than nine seconds. That's faster than the men's world record-holder for that distance. She would have been the Irish speed champion over 100 metres."

Bolt, from Jamaica, won the 100 metres in the Olympics in 2008 with a new world record speed of 9.69 seconds — but Kelly Ann would have been faster than his time.

But a defence expert quickly contradicted him — and said the police could simply not say what happened exactly.

And he added that he believed McArdle could have been telling the truth. "What Dermot McArdle is saying could be compatible with reality," he insisted.

It looked as if McArdle was finished. But then the state prosecutor intervened with devastating news for the Corcorans. He announced, out of the blue, that the state was withdrawing the murder charge. They no longer argued that he wanted to kill Kelly Ann — instead he killed her accidentally, and even tried to save her before she fell.

In a short summing up-speech, the prosecutor Yanez

Martinez told Judge Fernando Gonzalez: "The state maintains that around 7pm on February 11, 2000, the accused started a heated argument with his wife in the room of their hotel.

"That argument continued on the balcony where the accused increased his abuse to the point that he used force against her which induced her in the direction of the balcony in such a way that she went over the balcony and was left holding on to a handrail. The state maintains the accused tried to save his wife but she fell."

It was the worst possible news for the family. The state had been demanding McArdle be jailed for 14 years, but was now calling for him to be locked up for between two and four years. Under the Spanish system, the Corcorans were allowed to mount a parallel murder charge in their own right — which they continued with after the state withdrew its own case. But it was a massive setback nonetheless.

The obvious fear was the jury would accept the state's new case and conviction of the lesser charge of manslaughter.

That fear was realised the following Monday when after two days' deliberations, the jury acquitted him of murder — but convicted him of manslaughter.

The jurors, in their statement, accepted his claim he had tried to save his wife's life, but all nine branded him a liar by unanimously throwing out his claim that the mum-of-two died by accident after tripping as she tried to save Mark.

They attributed their guilty manslaughter verdict to McArdle's contradictory witness statements, in which he first claimed she killed herself, before bringing up the story about saving Mark. They also said they relied on police forensic evidence, concluding Kelly Ann could not have died as her husband claimed and evidence from Mr Haines, who said he spotted him lifting her above his head.

Despite being officially branded a wife-killer, McArdle was able to walk out of the front door of the court complex a free man. He lodged an immediate appeal and was let out on bail by the judge. A few minutes after he was declared a wife-killer, McArdle strode purposefully out of the court complex, his eyes covered by the sunglasses he wore in public every day of the trial. He didn't say a single word to waiting reporters.

But the Corcoran family were not so reserved. They had to sit through excruciating evidence in McArdle's trial —— including scandalous allegations that she was a bad drinker; that she wanted to go out drinking instead of looking after the son she adored; that she had had too much to drink the night she died. But the jury's verdict was clear — they simply did not believe McArdle's story.

More than eight years after her supposedly loving husband killed her during a row on a sun holiday, Kelly Ann Corcoran could finally rest in peace.

They had kept a dignified silence from the very first day, back in February 2000, that suspicions began to emerge that Kelly Ann's death was far from the accident her husband had claimed it to be.

They had steadfastly, but politely, declined to talk to the countless reporters who had called to their door over the previous eight years.

But now, finally, they had their chance to talk about the daughter and sister they missed so much.

Her brother-in-law Peter Moran, Caroline's husband and the man who had led the family's campaign for justice for eight long years, spoke for a few seconds outside the court following the verdict.

Fighting a losing battle to staunch the flow of tears, Mr Moran said: "We thank the people from Dundalk and the rest of Ireland for their best wishes and support. Most of all, we would like to thank St Gerard and Almighty God our Father for justice for Kelly Ann."

Later, speaking to *The Star*, in the Malaga hotel where the Corcoran family had been staying during the trial, Mr Moran said he had a simple message to McArdle — just say sorry. "Now that he has been convicted of killing Kelly Ann, he needs to be a man. He needs to admit what he has done wrong and he needs to say sorry." No such apology has ever been forthcoming.

As soon as the verdict came out, more details of McArdle's criminality emerged. It was revealed that in 1998 — two years before he killed Kelly Ann — he launched a vicious attack on a taxi driver in Dublin. The driver was punched so hard that muscles were torn in his head. "He planted me twice in the head through the open window," the driver recalled. "He hit me two digs full-on in the face with the force of his entire body behind him. I thought he'd broken my jaw — but the X-ray showed it was intact.

"But I was in severe pain because the force of the punches had torn the muscles on the opposite side of my face. When he had drink in him, he always got aggressive, but the way he acted that night, it would be fair to describe him as being like an animal."

The driver called gardai and McArdle was arrested. In September 1999, just five months before Kelly Ann's death, McArdle was convicted at Dublin District Court of assaulting the driver and was fine IR£250. The driver was suing him for compensation — but dropped the claim when he heard of the death of Kelly Ann, whom he knew.

"I lost my own stepson in a motorcycle accident that year — and I didn't want to add to the burden of someone who had suffered a similar tragedy," he explained.

Despite being convicted of killing his wife, McArdle was able to return home to his life in Ireland a few days after the jury gave its decision.

He must have been a confident man after Judge Gonzalez allowed him to leave Spain. Just 10 days later, that confidence was vindicated. The judge delivered his verdict — McArdle was handed a two-year prison sentence. The judge also ordered him to pay €220,000 in compensation. McArdle's two sons Mark and Paul, then aged 12 and 10, were to receive €60,000 each from their dad for the loss of their mum.

He was also ordered to pay Kelly Ann's parents Ted and Bridie some €100,000 in similar compensation.

McArdle must have been delighted. He knew that most cases in which someone has been sentenced in Spain to two or fewer years in prison — for a first offence — result in the entire term being suspended.

McArdle was back in Ireland just a few days after the conviction, but before his sentencing.

Life must have been looking up for the killer when news of the sentencing reached him. But, despite the probability he had avoided prison, he still lodged an appeal against the conviction. Early in 2009, however, he received hammer blow news that no-one had been expecting.

Shortly after the conviction, as Spanish law allows, lawyers representing Kelly Ann's family asked the judge not to suspend McArdle's jail term. There was, it seemed, very little chance of that request being accepted. All observers believed that he would order that the sentence be suspended, in line with standard practice for sentences of two years or fewer in Spain. But, on January 10, 2009, Judge Gonzalez agreed and ordered McArdle back to Spain to serve the two-year sentence in full. Within a few days, McArdle had lodged an appeal against that decision. But he failed in that and was again ordered to come back to Spain.

Once more, he appealed. Once more he failed. Just as he fought the law every step of the way before his conviction, so he did afterwards. He was determined not to go to jail and mounted legal challenge after legal challenge — even claiming the trial judge had discriminated against him by sending him to jail. A lengthy legal battle ensued, which kept McArdle in the headlines for weeks at a time.

But, in the meantime, he hit the news again — and for all the wrong reasons. In January, 2010 — more than a year after he was convicted — McArdle's partner Clare Dollard gave birth to the couple's first baby, a little girl.

Irish newspapers heard about the birth and staked out his home. McArdle saw photographer Jenny Matthews nearby and confronted her, demanding her camera. When she refused, he wrestled it from around her neck. The camera hit her in the face and she fell to her knees. "You're not so tough now without your camera," he told her, before walking off.

Ms Matthews called the Gardai, who contacted McArdle.

He denied any involvement, but later handed gardai the camera — with six images deleted. He was later found guilty, but was given a three-month suspended sentence.

That was the third criminal conviction he had received in two countries in just 11 years — and had yet to serve a single day behind bars for any of them.

Justice, however, finally caught up with Dermot McArdle on Saturday, January 29, 2011.

A few weeks earlier, with yet another appeal against his conviction and sentence in Spain, Judge Gonzalez had signed papers ordering him to Spain.

That document was then sent to the Spanish interior ministry who, following protocol, sent a request to the Irish Department of Justice, seeking McArdle's extradition under the European Arrest Warrant scheme. The department sent the request to the High Court, who rubber-stamped it and ordered his arrest.

That January morning, two detectives from the Garda Extradition Unit, based at the force's Phoenix Park headquarters, drove north and arrived at McArdle's home before 10am. But there was only one problem — he wasn't at home. Gardai then managed to make contact with him by telephone and he agreed to present himself to Dundalk Garda Station later that day. At around 11.30am, he was arrested and later driven to the High Court in Dublin, where the extradition order was agreed by Mr Justice Barry White.

But, true to form, McArdle — as is his right — launched an immediate appeal. He was taken to Cloverhill remand prison in west Dublin, where he spent several days before being released on bail. His appeal — his last chance to escape jail — was working its way through the Irish legal system in April and May this year, 2010.

Legal sources say the matter is likely to be resolved before the 12th anniversary of Kelly Ann's death, in February 2012. Then, and only then, will Kelly Ann be able to finally rest in peace.